THRIVING IN RETIREMENT

Ron,
I hope my book helps
you Thrive in Retirement,

A SYSTEM DESIGNED TO:

Outpace Inflation

Provide Income for Life

Reduce Stock Market Volatility

AVIVA PUBLISHING
NEW YORK

Jason R. Parker, CRFA™

Thriving in Retirement
A system designed to outpace inflation, provide income for life & reduce stock market volatility.
Copyright © 2011 by Jason R. Parker.

All rights reserved. No part of this book may be used or reproduced in any manner whatsoever without the expressed written permission of the author.

Address all inquiries to:
Jason R. Parker
9057 Washington Ave NW #104, Silverdale, WA 98383
360-337-2701 | info@parker-financial.net
www.parker-financial.net
www.thriving-in-retirement.com

Published by:
Aviva Publishing
Lake Placid, NY
518-523-1320
www.avivapubs.com

ISBN: 978-1-935586-28-9

Library of Congress Control Number: 2011924250

Editor: Tyler Tichelaar
Cover Photo: Gary Bowlby Photography
Cover, Jacket & Interior Book Design: Fusion Creative Works

Every attempt has been made to properly source all quotes.

Printed in the United States of America

First Edition

DISCLAIMER AND LIMIT OF LIABILITY

None of the material presented here is intended to serve as the basis for any financial decision, nor does any of the information contained within constitute an offer to buy or sell any security or insurance product. Such an offer is made only by prospectus, which you should read carefully before investing your money.

While the best efforts have been made in preparing this book, the author makes no representations or warranties with respect to the accuracy or completeness of this book's contents and specifically disclaims any implied warranties. The advice and strategies contained herein may not be suitable for your situation, and you should consult with a professional where appropriate.

This book contains performance data and some of this data is hypothetical in nature. Past performance does not guarantee future results. The data is provided solely for illustrative and discussion purposes. Please focus on the underlying principles.

The author's financial advice may change over time based on laws, regulations, tax codes, and experience. Therefore, you are encouraged to verify the status of the information contained in this book before acting.

Neither the author nor the publisher assumes liability or responsibility for any losses that may be sustained or alleged to be sustained, directly or indirectly, by the use of the information contained in this book, and any such liability is hereby expressly disclaimed.

For privacy reasons, the names of those whose stories are told have been changed for their protection.

DEDICATION

TO REBECCA, MY BEAUTIFUL WIFE AND BEST FRIEND:

Thank you for your love, kindness, and encouragement.
I am inspired by the life you lead.

TO OLIVER AND LIBBY, MY AWESOME CHILDREN:

The most important title I have ever had is Dad.
I hope I can live up to it.

TO MY PARENTS:

Thank you for your love, sacrifices, and teaching by example the meaning of hard work.

ACKNOWLEDGMENTS

Much of the success I have experienced wouldn't have been possible if it weren't for some very important people.

First, I have the greatest family a man could ever ask for. My wife, Rebecca, is my inspiration and encouragement. Without her I wouldn't have the great life I have today. She keeps me focused on what's truly most important in my life, which is my faith, family, and the relationships we create along the way. We have two beautiful, healthy, and vibrant children, and it's my greatest honor to hold the title of Dad.

Dean Schennum is an advisor with my firm. He has also been my mentor. He has more than thirty years of experience in the financial services arena, and without his guidance, support, insight, and sense of humor, Parker Financial never would have become what it is today.

Heather Henrichsen is my office administrator. Heather is brilliant and super-efficient and a great asset to our firm. Because of Heather's editing and journalism experience, this book is ten times better than it would have been.

No man is an island. I'd like to say that I created and engineered every system or concept you will read about in these pages. Unfortunately, that isn't the case. I surround myself with some of the top advisors in the country, and I am dedicated always to learning. My company would not be where it is today if it weren't for the opportunity to tap into the insight and experience of some of the greatest advisors in the country and for that I am grateful.

CONTENTS

Introduction: Core Concepts	9
Chapter 1: Conquering Change	21
Chapter 2: Focusing on What Is Most Important	29
Chapter 3: Saving Safely in Retirement	37
Chapter 4: Getting Your Legal House in Order	57
Chapter 5: Tax Planning	101
Chapter 6: Can I Afford to Retire?	107
Chapter 7: The Importance of Fees	131
Chapter 8: Diversifying in a Retirement Income Strategy	133
Chapter 9: Tips for Maximizing Your Social Security Benefit	139
Chapter 10: The IRA Legacy Optimizer	143
Chapter 11: Long-Term Care Insurance— Do You Really Need It?	149
Chapter 12: Paying Off Debt vs. SUPERSIZING Your Retirement Income	167
A Final Note: Thriving in Retirement	173
The Parker Financial Difference	175
About the Author	179

Introduction

CORE CONCEPTS

I often say I work with some of the greatest people in all of Kitsap County, Washington State, and perhaps the entire world. These people whom I serve daily have blessed me with their wisdom.

Below are some quotes and core concepts they've introduced me to that have shaped my life, this book, and my firm. This practical wisdom has kept my clients and our community "Thriving in Retirement."

- *The rich rule over the poor, and the borrower is slave to the lender.* — Proverbs 22:7

- *An investment in knowledge pays the best interest.* — Benjamin Franklin

- *It's not about how much you make; it's about how much you keep.* — Author Unknown

- Retirement is all about cash flow, not net worth.

- Pay your fair share of taxes, but not a penny more.

- *I'm more concerned with the return of my money than the return on my money.* — Will Rogers

- Cash is king, aka the Golden Rule: "He who has the gold makes the rules."

- *Debt is dumb.* — Dave Ramsey

- *Begin with the end in mind.* — Stephen Covey

- Don't confuse tax preparation with tax planning. Tax preparers are looking back, making sure the right numbers are in the right boxes. Tax planning is looking forward for ways to reduce your future tax liability.

- Don't put all your eggs in one basket. Diversify your time horizon as well as your investments.

- Seek independent, non-biased counsel that exercises fiduciary responsibility.

- Time is the cure to volatility in the stock market. Make sure time is on your side.

- Keep your fees low.

- One Momma can take care of eight babies, but eight babies can't take care of one Momma.

- Make your legacy about quality time spent with loved ones, not the money you leave behind.

- *Insanity: Doing the same thing over and over again and expecting different results.* — Albert Einstein

- Make Jesus the Lord and Savior of your life and put God first.

WHY YOU NEED THIS BOOK

The world has changed dramatically in the last couple of years. Our government is printing money at an unbelievable pace. Ten thousand baby boomers are retiring every day. Taxes are at historical all-time lows and likely to go up. Our national debt is, as I write this, currently more than 14 trillion dollars. Our government has recently bailed out financial institutions, taken over private companies, and has voted for one of the largest overhauls to our healthcare system in our country's history. The stock market's volatility is high, and what once appeared to be sage advice has turned into questionable theory. In fact, some people have recently said that "buy and hold" in the new economy should now be titled "buy, hold, and hope."

But more important than any of these external factors is making sure you have money for your retirement. If you are reading this book, then you are probably either just about to retire or already retired. While I certainly don't plan to fix all of the country's problems with this book, I do plan on giving you a system for getting the very most out of your retirement and helping you to implement a plan to achieve your retirement lifestyle goals with a high degree of confidence.

As the president of a wealth management firm that specializes in retirement, I have had the opportunity to meet with hundreds of people and help them on this very important journey into and through retirement. When I meet with people, they generally share the same five primary concerns:

- They never want to become a burden to their family either physically or financially.

- They don't want to run out of money before they run out of retirement.

- They want to pay in a legal manner as little in taxes as possible.

- They want to earn a fair rate of return on their money and outpace inflation with the least amount of volatility in their retirement portfolio.

- This last concern is probably the biggest one of all: They fear making an irreversible mistake.

Many of the people I meet tell me, "What I have is what I have." Now that they are no longer employed and not contributing to their retirement accounts, they feel concerned and restless about their investment decisions. Many prospective clients tell me they experienced a 30-60 percent decline in their investment values in 2008, and they don't want that type of volatility now that they are retired. *When did it become okay for retired people to be in situations where they could lose 50 percent of everything they have invested in one year?*

If you share in any of these concerns, then I'd encourage you to buy this book. At my wealth management firm, we are very specialized in the work we do, and because we are always researching the best academic and industry solutions to many of these issues, I want to share with you what I have learned through both my research and real-life experience.

Theory and practical application are two very different animals. A financial journalist talks about ideas that might work, but an advisor has worked with real people and real money to help them achieve their retirement goals. If financial journalists make mistakes, they can always retract or rewrite their opinions. But if retirement financial advisors make a mistake, the people they serve deal with devastating real-world consequences.

Being a financial advisor is a tremendous responsibility, and ultimately, people's welfare lies on the advisor's shoulders. That you are looking for sound financial advice is probably one reason you are reading this book. As an advisor who operates in a fiduciary capacity with the goal of always acting in my clients' best interests, I want to make sure I am doing my due diligence to ensure my clients are experiencing the desired outcome. I am more conservative than the average journalist or academic theorist because I have a lot more on the line than just selling a few books.

An old saying exists among the gardeners of life, "You want to be green and growing, not brown and wilting." To me, this philosophy means you must always be growing, learning, and challenging yourself because if you ever stop, you will wilt and die. I have the best intentions based on the best planning that I have discovered during my years in practice. I don't know of any better planning, but what works today may not be the best tomorrow. I am committed always to learning, discerning, and implementing what I believe are the best ideas available.

WHAT THIS BOOK IS NOT

A few years back, the furnace in my home broke, and I called a repairman to fix it. He was probably in his mid-sixties and very confident in his occupation. He popped the cover off the furnace and within twenty minutes had completely pulled my furnace apart, cleaned a few things, replaced a few pieces, and Shazam! He was done.

He handed me a bill for about $200 dollars. Talk about an hourly wage! Being the curious guy I am, I asked him what had been wrong with my furnace. He spent the next fifteen minutes talking to me in technical terms. He could have been speaking Japanese since it would have had the same impact on me. I just stood there nodding my head and wondering, "What in the world is this guy talking about?"

Now this gentleman was an expert, and he had probably forgotten more about my furnace than I will ever learn. That's exactly the kind of person I want to fix my furnace. I don't want to become a furnace repair expert, so I am willing to pay for his expertise. But at the same time, I realized he was assuming my level of knowledge was on par with his.

Unfortunately, I realize that many financial advisors assume the people they serve have the same level of comprehension on financial matters that they do. I spend up to ten hours a day working in my industry and learning the ins and outs of investing and all of the terminology that comes with it. But I can't expect my clients to have time to do the same. Therefore, this book is not a textbook for financial professionals. I am not trying to write a course for those who, like me, spend all of their days studying this industry.

This book is intended to share ideas, concepts, and strategies in a language that is relevant and accessible to the average person. While I will discuss some of the benefits of the work that financial advisors do, I won't spend a lot of time talking about the disadvantages. With any investment or insurance product, you need to understand all of the advantages and disadvantages before making a decision, and you should consult with a qualified advisor who can help you make sense of these ideas and lead you to understanding which ones may be best for your situation.

Every financial decision has positives and negatives. When it comes to your investments, you always get to choose from two of three possibilities:

- Rate of return
- Safety
- Liquidity

You can choose any two. If you want a high rate of return and liquidity, then you won't have safety. If you want safety and a high rate of return, then liquidity won't be an option. And if you want safety and liquidity, then you won't have a high rate of return.

I often have clients tell me their investment accounts are diversified. But what exactly does that mean? How do they know whether they are really diversified? Some of it depends on their definition of diversified. I believe that to be truly diversified means you have to be diversified in the following four areas:

- between "safe" and "growth" investment accounts across your whole investment portfolio,
- within your "growth" accounts in your portfolio,
- within your retirement **income** accounts in your portfolio, and
- between your "time horizon" and investment selections.

I'll discuss what each of these areas entails in future chapters.

Note: Some financial advisors will use the word laddering interchangeably with diversification.

DEFINITIONS

Let's take a moment and define a few terms you'll see pop up throughout this book.

- **Qualified accounts** are investment accounts where the taxes on the invested dollars and interest earned have NOT been paid yet. The most common examples are a 401k, a 403b, an Individual Retirement Arrangement (IRA), or an employer profit sharing plan. All of these plans work in the same basic way—money earned is invested into a qualified account on a pre-tax basis. Pre-tax basis means that no taxes have been paid and the investment earns interest over time on a tax-deferred basis. It also means you'll pay taxes on these funds when you pull them out, and they will be taxed at your ordinary income tax rates and your highest tax bracket when you do.

- **Non-qualified accounts** are those where taxes are paid prior to the investment being made. This scenario means you won't have to pay taxes on the principal again when you pull it out. You will pay taxes on any interest earned on these accounts, although this tax can be deferred until you actually pull it out of the account, depending on the financial tool you're using for investment.

- **Required Minimum Distribution (RMD)** is the minimum amount you must withdraw from tax-advantaged (qualified) retirement plans and accounts each year, beginning April 1 following the year you turn seventy-and-a-half, and by December 31 for subsequent years. These guidelines are established by the IRS and are subject to change.

- **Principal amount** is the money you originally invested before any interest or profit accrued. For example, if an investor's account were valued at $10,000 USD and he or she originally had invested $6,000 USD, the principal amount would be $6,000 USD. The remaining $4,000 USD would be the profit from the investments.

- **A 1099-INT or 1099-DIV (1099)** refers to a form that reports your interest or dividend income from investments reportable to the IRS as taxable income. Investment companies are required to send these forms to investors by the end of January every year.

- **Stock market indices** are the same as a stock market index. They are indices of market prices for a particular group of stocks, such as the S&P 500 and the Nasdaq Composite Index.

- **Mutual funds** are an open-ended fund operated by an investment company that raises money from shareholders and invests in a group of assets, in accordance with a stated set of objectives. Many types of mutual funds exist, including an aggressive growth fund, asset allocation fund, balanced fund, blend fund, bond fund, capital appreciation fund, clone fund, closed fund, crossover fund, equity fund, fund of funds, global fund, growth fund, growth and income fund, hedge fund, income fund, index fund, international fund, money market fund, municipal bond fund, prime rate fund, regional fund, sector fund, specialty fund, stock fund, and tax-free bond fund.

Throughout this book, we will look at these definitions and I'll give you more explanation of many of them. If need be, you can always turn back to this section for a reminder of the definition for each term.

You'll also find a complete listing of the links and resources found in this book at **www.thriving-in-retirement.com.**

Finally, before we get too far into the book, let me tell you a little about myself.

CONFESSIONS OF A FINANCIAL PLANNER

When you hear the word "confessions," automatically you think, "Oh boy, this is going to be good." Don't get too excited as my confessions are pretty GEEKY. I'm often asked, "How did you get started as a planner?"

That is actually a long story, but I will point out a couple of characteristics or quirks that work as an advantage in my profession. Having a degree in business administration and having experience in banking, insurance, and the investment field for more than ten years has contributed to my success, but the roots of that success go back even further.

When I was a young boy, my dad encouraged me to start a lawn mowing business. I went around to all of my neighbors and established accounts with a few of them. I soon had more work than I could handle so I hired some of my friends in the neighborhood to help. I was eleven years old when I started and moved from that neighborhood when I was twelve. When I was eighteen and just about to start college, I reconnected with a friend and found out the lawn mowing business I had started was still going strong. That was my first business, so watching it grow and knowing that it continued to thrive after I was gone was and still is an inspiration. Thanks, Dad.

I've always been a bit obsessive about my finances. When I would get my crusty dollar bills after mowing a lawn, I would take them home and wash them in the sink. I would lay them out on the counter and blow-dry them straight. I would bring them to the bank and deposit them in my savings account. At the time, that savings account was earning 10 percent. Ahh, the good old days.

I am also obsessed with numbers and counting. When I am driving down the highway, I count the number of tires on the vehicles driving in the opposite direction. Now this is pretty easy when you just have cars and trucks with four tires each, but when there are a lot of motorcycles and semi-trucks, it can really get your brain working quickly, not to mention that I am messing with the radio, wiping one of my kid's noses, handing the ChapStick to my wife and drinking a cup of coffee…just kidding.

One last little confession, and this one works into personal finance. I love budgeting. I know this really sounds weird to many of you, but I am the dorky guy in the checkout stand at the grocery store who has to input my debits into my iPhone and categorize the expenses. Let me tell you, this little quirk isn't very popular in the express lane. But when tax time comes, and my CPA asks me how much I spent, I just love pulling out my computer and giving her the exact number down to the penny.

Okay, you may be thinking I'm a bit quirky, but you need to keep track of your money, monitor it, and help it grow. You also need to make your money work for you so you don't have to work for your money. Keeping track of your expenses and investments as well as planning for the future will help you focus on what you enjoy. You don't have to become a financial advisor, just someone who takes an active interest in his or her finances. You probably already have that kind of interest or you wouldn't have picked up this book, so let's get started discovering how you can thrive in retirement.

Chapter 1

CONQUERING CHANGE

> *There is no shortage of knowing what to do;
> there is, however, a shortage of those willing to do.*
> — Author Unknown

In this book, I will show you how to create an investment strategy that reduces stock market volatility while providing growth, warding off inflation, and generating a lifetime cash flow.

Within the first five minutes of my educational seminars, I describe some of the common challenges or fears people have as they transition through retirement. The biggest is the "fear of making an irreversible financial mistake."

As people age and transition through retirement, their willingness and ability to change becomes more difficult. Fear paralyzes people into inaction. They will choose to do nothing rather than confront change. Most of the time, people don't make rational decisions about their finances or future, and that's unfortunate. Most of us tend to make emotional decisions about our money and lives. So when I present a client with a very rational reason to make a change such as diversification to reduce volatility, or using a tax-deferred or tax-free investment instead of a taxable investment, he may have a very difficult time making a decision even when the decision to change would greatly improve his situation.

One of my clients is currently eighty-nine years old. She has been widowed for years. When she was in her early eighties, her family encouraged her to move into a senior living facility. My client was opposed to this idea. She valued, as most of us do, her freedom and independence. Then a few years later, as she headed down the stairs in her home, she tripped and fell. She was in terrible pain. When I visited her in the nursing home, she told me her kids had been right and she was now going to move. Had she made the move earlier, perhaps she could have avoided this very unpleasant experience. I am happy to report that after a two-month recovery in the nursing home, she went home, packed up her life, and sold a bunch of stuff. She sold the home her husband and she had built, where they had raised their children and where she had lived for more than fifty years, and she moved into an independent senior living apartment complex. Talk about being brave.

I talk about change like it's something easy to do, but I can't imagine how hard that move must have been for her. Every time I speak with her now, she tells me how much she loves her life, and how moving out of her house was one of the best decisions she ever made. She talks about the freedom she has now to do more of what she truly enjoys, which in her case is painting and counseling. Change is the one constant in our lives, and no matter how comfortable we become, it will eventually sneak up on us and force us to grow.

The concepts I discuss in this book are going to challenge the way you have always done things. They may challenge conventional wisdom. They may challenge which investment vehicles or tools you use, and they will certainly rattle many of your most fundamental beliefs about how you have been growing and managing your money. I encourage you to let go of your pre-conceived ideas about finance and wealth management. Remember, retirement is a different animal. Even if you have accumulated great knowledge about creating wealth, a big difference exists between accumulating assets and the de-accumulation of assets. This book serves as a guide for the latter.

Education can be powerful, but only when it becomes an action. I dedicate time to writing every month, to offering free educational seminars, and to hosting Sound Retirement Radio to give people a greater understanding of the proper resources and tools available to them so they can make better decisions and become much more comfortable overcoming the hurdle of change.

Many of my clients are retired professionals. These sophisticated individuals have spent a lifetime developing their areas of expertise. Unfortunately and most admittedly, many of them have not had the inclination or the time to understand personal finance. Many of my clients tell me they have no desire to learn such things, so they've hired me as a professional to do it for them. Can you blame them? If I go to my doctor, I am relying on his years of expertise and training. It wouldn't make any sense for me to go back to medical school so I could spend all day diagnosing my health issues. At some point, you begin to realize that your time, not your money, is your most valuable asset, so how you spend that time becomes increasingly important as you transition through retirement.

The primary purpose of this book is to help retirees understand my system for diversifying their investment assets in retirement. My goal is simple:

- Protect assets from market volatility
- Keep assets growing to outpace inflation
- Provide income for life
- Overcome the hurdle of change

Retirement is about planning for the future, for the likely, and for the unexpected. Let me give you an example. In early 2008, I foresaw the economic downturn that was approaching and tried to warn my clients about it by sending them the following email.

January 18, 2008

Dear Client:

Given the state of our economy and the turbulent market conditions, I feel this message is important. Please be sure to read it and pass it on to your friends.

When I was three years old, I remember watching a cartoon where a rabbit was being chased by a hunter. The rabbit made his great escape by dropping a banana peel, and the hunter slipped and fell, giving the rabbit plenty of time to get away. Being the curious kid that I was, I ran off to the kitchen, grabbed a banana, and ate it as fast as I could. I walked over to the basement steps, set the banana peel down, and started pushing on it with my foot. Nothing happened. Being very persistent and determined, I reached down, turned the banana peel over, pushed it with my foot as hard as I could, and sure enough, those bananas really can be slick. I fell to the basement floor and split my head open. My dad picked me up and rushed me to the hospital. Several stitches and years later, you can still see the scar in the middle of my forehead.

What's the point you ask? Well, it sure looks like our economy is standing at the top of the steps with a banana under foot. If you haven't noticed the DJIA is down over 10 percent in the last three months. Heck, it's down almost 6 percent this year alone. That is only a small part of the problem. Our national debt, sinking dollar, slowing economy, and mortgage meltdown are just a few of the other issues, and the list goes on. Frankly, this problem has more to it than I'd like to talk about in this email.

Many people don't know there are savings vehicles out there that allow for market participation with no risk to principal. In other words, when the market is going up, you benefit, but when it's going down, you cannot lose your initial investment. In times of great uncertainty, it is important to help educate investors about all of their options.

These principal protected savings vehicles come in many different flavors. If you are an investor who shares some of my concerns, you may want to attend one of my free upcoming seminars. Visit www.parker-financial.net for more information. Feel free to call with questions.

*Hope all is well,
Jason Parker
President, Parker Financial*

I tried to warn my clients and community about the impending stock market blowup. I was able to help many people, but many did not heed the warning. My job is to keep a close eye on my clients' retirement funds and investments. That's what I do, and I work hard to keep my community and clients up to speed with what's happening. "You can lead a horse to water, but you can't make it to drink." You are, ultimately, the one who has to make the hard decisions. So you have to ask yourself, "Do I really want financial help?"

I struggle with change as much as the next person. When my wife and I go out to dinner, we will go to the same restaurant because it is familiar to us. If I buy a bottle of wine, I usually go with the wine I know I like. When we go to Hawaii for vacation, we often revisit the same place. It's comfortable and safe, and we know what to expect.

Challenge yourself to embrace change. Go out to dinner tonight to a restaurant where you have never been. Start a new exercise class or join a new gym. Instead of just listening to everyone else sing at church on Sunday morning, let loose and give it your all. Do something that gets you out of your comfort zone. It will be a good exercise for you to take small steps toward change before you take the hard steps toward changing your money habits.

I recognize that changing your finances or your advisor may be a scary endeavor. And if you are happy with the results you are getting, maybe you won't need to make a change. But if you are unhappy with either the relationship you have or the results you are getting, please don't accept mediocre or poor results just because change is hard. One reason I enjoy working with retirees is because of the wisdom they bring to our relationship. I am grateful to have people in my life like the eighty-nine year old woman whose story I told above because she is a reminder and inspiration to me about what can be accomplished. Yes, change can be scary, but even scarier is staying in a sinking ship. If the situation warrants it, be prepared to make a change.

Chapter 2

FOCUSING ON WHAT IS MOST IMPORTANT

One of my clients once said to me, "I can spend my time losing money in the stock market, and I can spend my time making the money back in the stock market. But once I spend my time, I can never get it back."

This chapter is extremely important because it's about focusing on what is most valuable in your life, namely:

- spending your time with those you love
- learning to appreciate what you have
- being grateful
- finding peace
- being involved in your community
- taking time to pray and worship, and
- being that incredible parent, grandparent, and friend.

If you don't have your priorities straight at this stage in life, you better get going because you may not have time on your side. Many of my clients come to realize their most precious asset is their time.

They could probably manage their money just as well as I can. But they don't want to do it. They want to live, and so they learn to outsource the mundane details like money management. I am not suggesting you close your eyes, hand over all your money, and forget about it. You still need to be prudent, meet regularly with your advisor, and ask a lot of questions. But chances are that if you are like most of my clients, you haven't envisioned your retirement years as sitting in front of a computer and placing stock trades all day long.

People have a lot of different reasons for hiring a money management firm or financial advisor. Sometimes it's because they don't want to become subject matter experts. Sometimes they already are experts, but they want to create the relationship to make sure that if anything happens to them, a trusted backup person is in place. Sometimes, they choose a financial advisor just to simplify their lives. When it's time to retire, some people are ready to put their feet up and relax.

You will pay fees depending on the level of service you would like. Be sure you find an advisor who provides you with the different pricing options you might want to consider.

- **Fee for planning.** In this type of arrangement, you pay your advisor a fee once per year to review your portfolio and make any suggestions and recommendations. You get a second set of eyes to look things over and make sure you aren't missing anything. Depending on the complexity of your situation, this fee will likely range anywhere from $99-$10,000.

- **Investment Management.** This style of management is appropriate for people who don't want to do all of the buying and selling required with investments. They are looking for a money manager who will watch their accounts daily and make adjustments as needed. Many of the people I meet with in retirement feel this assistance is prudent to have since they are no longer contributing to their retirement assets. They want an extra level of oversight to make sure their investment accounts are being optimized. You should expect to pay anywhere from 0.5 to 2 percent annually depending on the size and complexity of your accounts. Sometimes a fee-based management firm will accept commissions as a part of its compensation. This situation can be okay as long as it is disclosed upfront. In my experience, mixing fees and commissions on products has been one way to reduce the overall cost to you.

- **Commission only.** In this scenario, the planner works on commission only. I'd stay away from this type of relationship. Not because the planner is a bad person, but because it creates a conflict of interest for you that may not serve you the best. If the advisor only gets paid for selling you something, you may end up with a wonderful experience when you first start, but overtime, you may begin to feel that the advisor just doesn't have time for you. If the advisor only gets paid when he or she sells you a product, then you will always wonder, "Is this really the best for me or is it the best for my advisor?" Stay away from working with people who are commission-only salespeople.

I have a small firm that offers a very high level of service, and I intend to keep it that way. I would much rather do a very good job for a small group of people than a mediocre job for a large group of people.

One of my prospective clients delivered a book to my office a few years back. It was *The Seven Habits of Highly Effective People* by Stephen Covey. The first few pages of the second chapter of this book changed my life.

Stephen Covey introduces the principal of "begin with the end in mind" and he takes the reader through a very powerful visualization exercise. He asks you to close your eyes and imagine you just pulled up to a church. You walk inside the church and realize you are at a funeral. You walk to the front of the room look in the casket and realize it's YOU. You sit down in the front row and for the next hour you listen as co-workers, family members, your spouse, children, and community all celebrate your life. The two questions I contemplated while going through this exercise were:

- How will I be remembered?

- What have I contributed?

By figuring out what my answers currently were, and then figuring out what I wanted the answers to be, I was able to define what was most important to me, and then I started taking the steps to get me there.

Here is what I mean when I say, "Focus on what's most important." When your grandson gets up at your funeral to talk about the legacy you left, my hope is that it will be about the life lessons you taught him out on the river fishing. Nobody ever stands up and says, "My grandpa sure had a great 401k, and it was so great watching him spend all day and night reviewing his statements."

Focus on what's most important in your life and hire experts to take care of the details so you can answer the two questions above without hesitation or delay the way you want them to be answered: *"How will I be remembered?"* and *"What have I contributed?"*

LEAVING A LEGACY

I remember the time I received a call from one of my client's daughters to let me know her mom had died. My client was a very nice person with an inviting smile who was always helping her family and community. I had visited her several times in the weeks leading up to her death. The very last time I had met with her, she was no longer able to move from her chair without assistance. She said to me with her voice trembling, "I don't have much time left." She had asked me to review her estate and financial plans one last time. She wanted to know that when she was gone, her family would be taken care of financially.

My client loved to knit, sew, and crochet. She had four children and many grandchildren. She and her husband had been very successful in business and they had raised a very close family. Whenever any of her kids or grandkids married, she would make the new couple a beautiful quilt. To accommodate all the guests, her funeral was held in a local school gymnasium. At her funeral, her friends and family draped the quilts she had made along every wall.

The thought of her legacy continues to touch me, and it reminds of what is truly important in this life. Her faith, family, and community were her highest priorities. What may surprise you is that she also left her family a fairly large estate. But at the celebration of her life, dollar bills were not hanging from the walls—quilts were. Beautiful, handmade, exquisite quilts she had poured her heart into. That, my friends, is the type of legacy I hope all of my clients will leave.

While people make all kinds of plans and preparations to leave money, to simplify or to maximize their estates, they forget the most valuable pieces of their legacies: their personal stories of their triumphs and greatest achievements. Oftentimes, all that is left are the pictures of people's lives, the careers they had, the dates and times they lived, but their stories are lost.

I know the Bible speaks about leaving a financial legacy, and I understand that importance, but the financial inheritance is actually the easier part. What's not so easy is taking the time to sit down and share your story. Today, the process is getting easier because of online blogs and dictation software that allow you to speak words into your computer rather than type. Let me encourage you to leave a grand legacy, one that will live forever and be more valuable to future generations than simply leaving money.

When I was twenty-one, I moved out of my dad's house. I had been dating Rebecca for more than two years. I knew she was the one for me, but she had recently moved to Alaska to finish getting her bachelor's degree. So as soon as I graduated, I decided to follow her and her family to Juneau, Alaska.

I was planning to drive from California to Seattle to put my car on the barge. I had packed all of my belongings into a large duffle sack and put a Jim Croce tape in the car for the long drive. It was really an adventure. I had said all of my goodbyes to my family and was getting into my car when my Dad came outside. With tears welling up in his eyes, he gave me a big hug and said, "Good

Luck." Then he reached into his pocket and pulled out a silver dollar. It was dated the same year as my birth. He pressed the silver dollar into the palm of my hand and said, "Jason, since I moved out of my home, I have never had to go to my family for money. I've done it on my own, but I wanted to give you this silver dollar just in case things ever get tight."

Rebecca and I got married a few years after I joined her in Alaska, and we have been together ever since. We, like many people, made our mistakes with money. It's an important part of the learning process. Someone once said, "If you aren't making mistakes, you aren't living."

I am very proud of the fact that I have never had to go to my family for money. I still have the silver dollar my Dad gave me years ago. There have been times when things got pretty tough for us, but that silver dollar meant so much more than just the money it was worth.

During my years of helping people plan for retirement, I have seen many families torn apart by an inheritance. I have seen brothers fall out of good favor with one another, and sisters who will no longer speak to each other because of money. One of the greatest joys in my life has been learning how to become successful financially without receiving help from family or having to wonder what I will get from them.

I do not plan to leave a lot of money to my children or grandchildren because I would hate to rob them of the awesome experience of learning how to win at the game of life. And I certainly would be deeply troubled if my children fell out of favor with one another because of a large inheritance.

I suggest that you spend your money while you are alive. Create memories. Take your family on vacations and cruises. Take them out to eat. Spend the holidays with them. Create the relationships and share your wisdom. More importantly, give them the most valuable gift of all: your time.

Plan to leave your loved ones some money, but not so much that it cripples their abilities to grow on their own.

Chapter 3

SAVING SAFELY IN RETIREMENT

Now that you know how important it is to focus on the future, not only for your own retirement, but so you can leave a legacy to your family, you need to learn how to make the money you have last throughout your retirement. The last thing you want to do is run out of money before you run out of life, and if you don't plan carefully, in today's economy, that scenario can become a very real possibility.

SENIORS ARE BEING SQUEEZED

Senior citizens are being squeezed, and I'm not talking about bear hugs from the grandkids. Higher property taxes along with inflation are driving up the costs of gasoline, food, healthcare, and insurance. Couple these with a very volatile stock market, longer life expectancies, and declining yields on fixed income investments, and we have an especially alarming trend for folks who are retired.

When people retire, they shift from a strategy of accumulating assets to a strategy of preserving and distributing the assets they have accumulated. Certificates of Deposit (CDs) seem to be a popular safe haven for many of these folks. While CDs certainly offer a great deal of safety, another alternative does exist.

After a quick visit to **www.bankrate.com**, I noticed that the overnight national average yield on a five-year CD is currently 3.24 percent. Assuming these are taxable dollars, it would be prudent to calculate your yield after tax. So if you are in the 25 percent marginal tax bracket, the after tax yield on your CD is only 2.43 percent. Then factor in a conservative estimate of 3 percent for inflation, and you can see inflation and taxes are taking a big bite out of your bottom line. Your principal is safe from market volatility, but not from taxes and inflation.

A common tax planning strategy is to defer income from the current year to later years because a dollar in hand today is worth more than a dollar in the future: the time value of money. This concept is particularly important during inflationary times.

So what is the other alternative to CDs, and how can you defer the tax on interest earned from your CD? One often overlooked and misunderstood savings vehicle is the tax-deferred fixed-rate annuity. One of the reasons insurance companies created tax-deferred fixed-rate annuities was to compete for the dollars currently invested in CDs. These tax-deferred fixed-rate annuities work in much the same way that CDs work with respect to how they credit interest, but the annuities offer a few advantages not found in CDs.

First, and probably the most obvious, is they are tax deferred. You won't receive a 1099 interest statement at the end of every year for the interest you earn in your annuity, as long as the interest isn't withdrawn from the annuity. Second, the rates are currently higher than the national average for CDs. As of this morning, I noticed an offering of 5.30 percent fixed for five years for deposits over $100,000. Remember, these fixed-rate annuities are tax deferred so the taxable equivalent needed by a CD would be 7.07 percent. Or in real dollars, $100,000 invested in a 5-year CD at 3.24 percent in a 25 percent marginal tax bracket, assuming you are paying your taxes from the interest earned each year, would have a value of $112,755.01 at the end of five years.

The tax-deferred fixed-rate annuity would have a value of $129,461.88 at the end of the same five year period. At the end of the five year annuity contract, you can continue to defer your taxes out into the future by doing what is called a 1035 exchange to another fixed rate annuity. Unlike IRA's, you don't have to begin taking a required minimum distribution at age seventy-and-a-half. Unless of course you have an annuity inside your IRA; then the IRA rules override the annuity rules.

As with CDs, you may pay a penalty for drawing funds out of your deferred annuity before the end of the five-year period. Taxes can be deferred as long as you are alive and continue to 1035 exchange the contracts, but when you start to take the money out of the annuity, you will have to pay taxes at ordinary income tax rates. Annuities are offered by insurance companies so you need to know and understand the financial strength of the insurance company offering the annuity.

If you invest in CDs and don't need the interest income for current living expenses, you may want to consider the benefits of a tax-deferred fixed-rate annuity as an alternative.

SAFETY—WHAT DOES IT MEAN TO YOU?

In my first meeting with prospective clients, I ask, "How much of your money do you want safe?" Most people have a hard time answering this question because they would like more safety, but still want to outpace inflation.

The root of this question is the word "safe." What does that word mean to you? It means different things to different people. At my firm, "safety" is not being able to lose your principal based on market fluctuations and always being able to calculate your worst case scenario when you need access to your money.

By using my definition for safety, it really narrows the tools I will use to fill this segment of a retirement strategy.

Many people do not really understand bonds and categorize them as "safe." Folks, bonds do not work if you subscribe to my definition of safe because we don't know what the worst case future scenario will be if we have to liquidate the bond before maturity, this applies even with U.S. Treasury bonds. At least with a corporation, we have the ability to review their books to see whether they are worthy of an investment.

But the way our country is printing money and using creative math, it's hard to determine whether U.S. Treasury bonds are a good deal. U.S. Treasury bonds are the safest when held to maturity compared to any other bonds available, but if you have to liquidate your bond before maturity, it is possible to lose money on U.S. Treasury bonds depending on market conditions.

Let's take a quick minute to explore the three different vehicles that I believe are truly safe, secure and guaranteed.

- **Certificates of Deposit** are offered by banks and are commonly known as CDs. As long as you are working with a bank that is FDIC insured, and you are below the FDIC insurance limits, you should feel safe owning these instruments.

- **Fixed Deferred Annuities** are offered by insurance companies. They work in much the same way as CDs do because they pay a fixed rate of interest. Fixed deferred annuities are NOT FDIC insured. The first line of defense is to make sure you are working with a highly rated insurance company. They should be at least A- rated by AM Best. But if an insurance company should fail, most fixed annuities are guaranteed by your state's guarantee association. You can check how much of your principal is protected from loss by visiting **www.NOHLGA.com**, but in most instances the guarantee covers $100,000.

- **U.S. Savings Bonds** are backed by the U.S. Government so if our country were to fail, you might lose your principal. If the U.S.A. fails, then your money probably won't be worth anything anyway. Unlike treasury bonds whose price will fluctuate with market conditions (interest rates), your savings bonds avoid that risk. One popular variation of the savings bond is the I Bond. The I Bond is a savings bond that pays interest, which is, in part, based on inflation. Unfortunately, how we calculate inflation these days is getting a little skewed. I can't understand why the cost of food and energy isn't included when determining inflation. Isn't that where most of us spend our money?

All three of these vehicles pay a fixed rate of interest. They have competitive rates, and you should never have to pay a commission to invest your money in any of them. Generally speaking, CDs, fixed annuities, and savings bonds all carry a penalty if you withdraw your money before maturity. But you always know your worst case scenario if you have to liquidate the holding before maturity. And because of the underlying guarantees, you know your principal is safe even if the bank or insurance company were to go under.

Depending on whether you will be withdrawing the interest for income or just reinvesting the interest from your investments may have an impact on which of the above tools you use.

Using CDs for non-qualified accounts has a disadvantage because you are taxed on your interest income even if you don't use it. That pesky 1099 will show up at the end of the year, and you will have to pay tax on your interest income.

Fixed deferred annuities and savings bonds both offer tax deferral, even in non-qualified accounts. So you control when you pay taxes. By controlling your tax liability, you have the opportunity to benefit from triple compounding: compounding on your interest, compounding on your principal, and compounding on your tax savings.

Obviously, the time value of money concept is applied here. The good folks at **www.investopedia.com** have this to say about it: "This core principal of finance holds that, provided money can earn interest, any amount of money is worth more the sooner it is received. This concept is also referred to as the present discount value."

The bottom line is: I want you to pay your fair share in taxes, but I want you to be in control of when you pay those taxes. I want you to be on the winning side of the "time value of money" concept and not the government.

Be sure to use a trusted third-party custodian for your investments, so you don't end up in a Bernie Madoff scam. (Bernie Madoff operated the largest Ponzi scheme in history. A Ponzi scheme is a fraudulent investment operation that pays returns to separate investors, not from any actual profit earned by the organization, but from their own money or money paid by subsequent investors.)

A custodian acts as the intermediary between you and your advisor. I currently work with Fidelity and Folio Institutional for my clients. My clients' investment accounts are housed at these custodians. I have the ability to place trades in these accounts, but I cannot withdraw money from the accounts other than my fee for being their financial advisor. Only the client can access these accounts. This limited access provides an extra layer of protection for the client. Had the poor folks whom Madoff ripped off been using a third-party custodian, he wouldn't have been able to get away with what he did. Custodians mitigate the risk of dishonest activity by separating the fund managers from the physical securities and investor records.

BANKS AND FINANCIAL RATINGS

IndyMac Bank was seized by federal regulators in what was called, "The second largest bank failure in U.S. history." Thank goodness the FDIC exists to help protect deposits. With all of the turmoil in the financial sector, my clients want to know about the financial strength of their banks. According to the FDIC website:

The FDIC never releases its ratings on the safety and soundness of banks and thrift institutions to the public. As a service to consumers, the staff of the FDIC Library has compiled a listing of several financial institution rating services. Disclaimer: This list should not be construed as an endorsement or confirmation by the FDIC of information provided by these companies.

I clicked on several of the different rating agencies listed by the FDIC. The one I found easiest to navigate was offered by Bauer Financial at www.BauerFinancial.com. It offers a free rating report for banks and credit unions. And to keep the legal beagles happy, I will restate the following disclaimer: Parker Financial LLC does not endorse or confirm the information provided by Bauer Financial.

When a bank fails, you will hear stories about people whose money was not covered by FDIC insurance because they were over the limits. Go to www.fdic.gov to review the FDIC's frequently asked questions, which should help clarify what is and is not covered by FDIC.

KEY RATING RESOURCES

- Visit AM Best at **www.ambest.com** to check on the financial strength of the insurance company offering your annuity.

- Visit Treasury Direct at **www.treasurydirect.gov** for buying your U.S. Savings bonds and I Bonds.

- Visit Bauer Financial at **www.bauerfinancial.com** to check on the financial strength of your bank.

- For a complete listing of the links and resources found in my book, please visit **www.thriving-in-retirement.com**

BONDS—WHAT KEEPS ME UP AT NIGHT

I hate to toot my own horn, but as you saw from the email I sent to my clients in 2008, I warned about our economy falling off a cliff very early on. They say hindsight is 20/20, and we can all look back now at the housing bubble and think, "I should have known it was coming." Of course, financial advisors all try to recognize trends early so they can position their clients before things get too ugly. When I shine up my crystal ball, here is what I see happening in the future.

Bonds are often touted as a safe alternative to stocks. Recent articles and evidence have suggested that bonds are safer than stocks over the long haul. However, bonds carry a substantial amount of risk and should not be discussed as safe. If you can lose money due to market volatility, then it is not safe.

Bonds have several different risks including default risk, credit risk, and call risk to name a few. I am going to discuss what I believe is the **most obvious risk of all right now—interest rate and term/maturity risk.** Bonds have a direct relationship with interest rates. If you buy a bond today, and it is paying an interest rate of 4 percent, but tomorrow the interest rates go up, so you could now buy a bond at 5 percent, then you could potentially lose money on the bond you purchased yesterday at 4 percent interest if you had to liquidate the bond before maturity.

Why would anyone want to buy a 4 percent bond from me when he could buy a bond from the issuer at 5 percent? Well, they won't want to buy your bond at 4 percent unless you discount the price. When you discount the price, it means you may receive less than your original investment back in return. If you hold a bond today and interest rates go up, your bond will be worth less money if you have to sell your bond before its maturity.

The question to ask is, "Are interest rates going to stay flat, go down, or go up in the future?" Take a look at a historical chart of the federal funds rate below before answering this question. The federal funds rate is the interest rate at which private depository institutions (mostly banks) lend balances (federal funds) at the Federal Reserve to other depository institutions, usually overnight. It is the interest rate banks charge each other for loans.

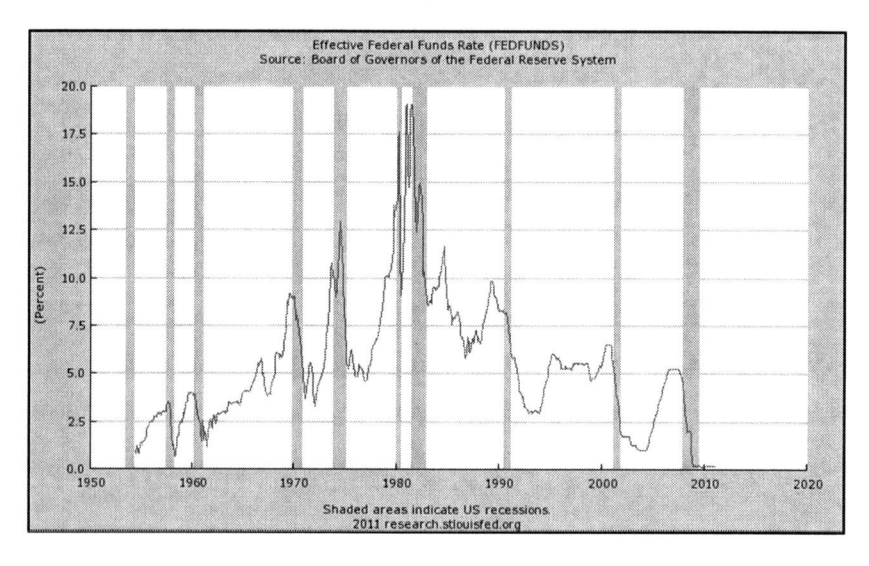

The U.S. Federal Government is printing money like crazy. Interest rates are at a historical all time low, and less demand is being seen at U.S. Treasury auctions, both of which are causing interest rates to rise. Right now these factors are all pretty subtle. Even though the media is giving the matter plenty of coverage, it seems like people aren't paying attention.

In the early 1970s, the stock market crashed. The Dow Jones Industrial Average (DJIA) fell 45 percent. That was a doozie. Prior to the crash, the federal funds rate was at 12 percent. The federal funds rate is one way our government influences short-term interest rates and encourages economic growth. By lowering the rate, the government allowed for cheaper borrowing, which in turn should have stimulated the economy.

By 1976, the federal funds rate had plunged from 12 percent to less than 6 percent. Why is this important? How do people react after they lose 45 percent in a stock market selloff? They go to their broker and say, "Mr. Broker, I want more safety." So the broker, following the common wisdom that bonds are safer than stocks, rebalances the client's portfolio and puts more money in bonds and less in stocks.

But by 1981, the federal funds rate had skyrocketed to 18 percent. So even though you were buying bonds for more safety in 1976, you were buying in at 6 percent or less. A few years later, you could buy bonds that were paying 18 percent or more. If you had to liquidate your 6 percent bonds before maturity, you would have taken a great big bath. And if you didn't liquidate the bonds, you saw all of your friends earning three times the yield. Bonds are not as safe as you might think.

Fast forward to 2007. The federal funds rate in 2007 was 4 percent before the market crashed, and now it floats from 0 percent to 0.25 percent. People are going to their brokers and saying, "I want more safety." You can see where this is going. The broker rebalances the client's portfolio to a stronger bond position and.... Well, the future has yet to happen, but folks, if I were a betting man, I'd have to bet interest rates are going to be higher in the future. Remember, if interest rates go up and you hold a bond, the value of your bond is likely to go down. You could recognize a loss if you had to liquidate that bond before maturity.

One of the primary reasons I believe interest rates are going to go up is because of the continued lack of interest in the treasury offerings. Let's face it. We need foreign nations to finance all of the spending we are doing. These countries are not very excited about buying a 30-year treasury bond that is paying 4 percent when our dollar is down the tubes and losing ground as we continue to print money. The solution: The U.S. will have to raise interest rates to continue to attract capital from our foreign financiers.

So what can you do about it? If you are looking for more safety, you must use safe money alternatives. Remember how I define safe. Safe is something that is guaranteed, and you always know your worst case scenario.

We can use bonds as a negatively correlated asset class to stocks to offset your portfolio for your at-risk and market sensitive investments, but bonds are not the safest place for your money to be either. Always remember to ask about the term of the bond. If you are retired and are seventy years old, do you really want to buy a twenty-year bond?

Don't fool yourself about the strength of the company in which you are investing. Things change. What you may perceive as a strong company today may not look too good in just a few years. Just look at Chrysler, Lehman Brothers, Enron, GM, Worldcom, Bear Stearns, and Washington Mutual.

Should you own bonds in a **well diversified at-risk investment** portfolio? Answer: Yes.

Just remember you can lose money in bonds, so they should be used with caution and should be considered an at-risk investment rather than a safe one.

Two very important terms you should familiarize yourself with if you are going to invest in bond mutual funds are:

- Average Effective Duration
- Average Effective Term/Maturity

Average effective duration essentially measures interest rate sensitivity. The longer the duration, the more volatility you can expect. A portfolio that has an average duration of twenty years would be twice as volatile as a portfolio with an average duration of ten years.

Average effective maturity measures the weighted average of all the maturities within the portfolio.

It is critical that you know and understand both of these numbers. If you currently hold bond mutual funds, please contact a financial advisor who will run reports to help you uncover and decipher this information.

Why do we diversify among stocks and bonds? Stocks provide for growth, and our hope and goal for growth is generally 10-12 percent. We are willing to take risk with stocks because our hope is to outpace inflation over a long period of time, and stocks have a decent record for helping to accomplish that.

Bonds, on the other hand, are usually purchased to smooth volatility in a stock portfolio and generate income. Generally, the return that we expect from bonds will range from 3-6 percent.

You should use the right tool for the job. You need to ask yourself these three questions: Are bonds the best way to accomplish a desired 3-6 percent return? Are bonds the best tool for smoothing portfolio volatility? How can we generate income with less risk and more tax efficiency?

These are three distinct and very different objectives, and if your primary goal is a return of 3-6 percent, better tools than bonds exist. And if your primary goal is a return of 3-6 percent with less risk in an attempt to smooth volatility, then better alternatives exist for that as well. If your goal is a tax efficient guaranteed income, then a better tool for that objective also exists given the 0 percent interest rate environment we live in.

BONDS VS. FIXED INDEXED ANNUITIES

A Fixed Indexed Annuity is a contract with an insurance company that offers some unique features and is a safe alternative to bonds. Fixed Indexed Annuities (FIAs):

- are considered a safe place for money.

- are guaranteed against loss of principal.

- guarantee a minimum rate of return/worse case.

- have the ability to earn a return greater than the minimum guarantee based on the upward movement of a stock market index such as the S&P 500 or the DJIA.

- give you greater control of your tax liability with the available tax deferral option.

- ends at death so your beneficiaries receive the account value without having to hold the position until maturity like they would have to do with a bond.

- when structured properly, will bypass probate and go directly to your named beneficiaries.

- have liquidity features allowing you to access your account value at any time. Ninety percent of your money is usually available while 10 percent could be eaten up by surrender charges if you were to pull all of your money out in the first year. On the flip side, you can access 10 percent of the account value every year without any type of surrender charge or penalty. This advantage makes them a little more attractive than most CDs.

FIAs offer many attractive features for the average retiree. Now, downsides do exist for these tools, so you should request the product brochures and know the financial strength of the company issuing them before you make a decision.

With interest rates at an all time low, if you invest in a bond today and interest rates go up, you could lose principal if you had to sell your bond before maturity, or, in these volatile times, if you own an individual bond and that company fails, you could lose your principal.

Because Fixed Indexed Annuities will credit interest based on the stock market's movement, they can be a good alternative to a bond portfolio. In a 2009 interview with *Annuity Digest*, David Babbel, a Wharton Professor who had recently conducted a study about FIAs, stated:

> The in-depth studies we conducted took over two years to complete and involved six Ph.D. financial economists and a pair of very well known senior actuaries. Our studies show that the products of at least some of the companies in this field are viable—indeed, rather attractive products. Our findings regarding actual products show that since their inception in 1995, they have performed quite well—in fact, some have performed better than many alternative investment classes (corporate and government bonds, equity funds, money markets) in any combination.[1]

As I researched FIAs, I came across an October, 2009 report titled "Real World Index Annuity Returns" by the Wharton Financial

---

[1] http://www.annuitydigest.com/blog/tom/interview-wharton-professor-david-babbel-part-one Accessed February 12, 2011.

Institutions Center. The paper was written by David Babbel, as well as Jack Marrion and Geoffrey VanderPal. Now these guys have some pretty impressive credentials. Jack Marrion is an MBA doctoral candidate in the area of cognitive bias in decision-making and is president of Advantage Compendium. Geoffrey VanderPal, DBA, MBA, CLU, CFS, RFC, CTP, CAMS, is the Chief Investment officer of Skyline Capital Management. David Babbel is a professor of insurance and finance at the Wharton School of Business, University of Pennsylvania, a Senior-Advisor to Charles River Associates, and a fellow of the Wharton Financial Institutions Center.

The entire report is very interesting and available online for download at the Wharton Financial Institutions Center's website.[2]

Page 6 of this report, paragraph 4, states, "From 1997 through 2007 the five-year annualized returns for FIAs averaged 5.79 percent. This compares to 5.39 percent for taxable bond funds and 4.73 percent for fixed annuities."

These numbers were based on actual customer statements and from a limited number of contracts. You should read this report in its entirety, but what is important is that it provides information on how these contracts actually performed—not how they hypothetically would have performed.

Here are some important questions to ask yourself: Has your advisor ever mentioned this type of product to you? And do you currently own bonds or bond mutual funds in your investment portfolio?

---

2   http://fic.wharton.upenn.edu/fic/Policy%20page/RealWorldReturns.pdf Accessed February 12, 2011.

The reality is that these tools, when utilized properly, can provide an alternative to a bond portfolio. My experience tells me that many advisors don't make these tools available to their clients. But it's not the advisors faults. Many of the folks in my community work for large Wall Street-owned corporations that determine what is and what is not available for their clients.

My guess is that these firms cannot make enough money selling these products so they don't make them available to their advisors to offer to clients.

For this reason, I believe you should choose to work with an independent advisory firm that acts in a fiduciary capacity by conducting business or handling property for the benefit of another person. The advisors are responsible for proving, if asked, that they acted in their clients' best interests, not their own. Many independent advisory firms are registered investment advisors (RIAs). RIAs are registered with the U.S. Securities and Exchange Commission, which manages the investments of others. This registration doesn't mean the advisor is recommended by the SEC, but it means he or she is regulated by the SEC. In general, an RIA with more than $25 million under management must register with the SEC. RIAs managing less than $25 million are registered at the state level.

By working with an independent advisory firm that is an RIA, you know you are working with a firm that will always work in your best interest, and because of its independence, it will have access to all of the products available and not just those the corporation allows.

UNDERSTANDING THE SPIA

An SPIA is a Single Premium Immediate Annuity contract. These contracts have been designed by insurance companies to provide a guaranteed income stream. Chances are, if you have a pension from your employer, you already have an SPIA. The company most likely purchased an insurance contract that guarantees your monthly income payments for the remainder of your life. SPIAs are one of the most underutilized annuity contracts. The academic world has long sung their praises and the U.S. Government is encouraging retirees to use a portion of their retirement accounts to fund these contracts.

An SPIA insures against an individual outliving his or her retirement income. SPIAs can be structured to provide a guaranteed income for a surviving spouse as well. SPIAs are offered by insurance companies; in a recent interview with a very large insurance company, the insurance company representative said people used to go to insurance companies to help protect against the risk of dying too soon. Now insurance companies are helping to protect against the risk of living too long.

According to a Fidelity Investments report based on the 11 million 401k plans it manages, the average 401k balance dropped 31 percent from the end of 2007 to the end of March 2009. The S&P 500 tumbled 46 percent during that same period. Retirement is all about cash flow, not net worth. If you have a million dollars invested in the S&P 500 and you are pulling money from it for income, and your account drops 46 percent in one year, you will have some sleepless nights. An SPIA, if set up properly, could guarantee between 60-100 percent of your income without having to rely on the stock market. Then when the volatile stock market drops, it won't be such a shock to your system.

SPIAs are probably underused because they don't pay a very large commission to the agents who sell them. A bond portfolio, on the other hand, allows for ongoing management fees to generate revenue for the brokers and brokerage firms selling them.

The income you receive from a non-qualified SPIA account is also split by an exclusion ratio. A portion of the money is considered a return of premium and a portion of it is considered taxable interest income. SPIAs are very tax-efficient at creating income, and in today's interest rate environment, they are much safer than a bond portfolio. Bonds, of course, receive poor tax treatment since the interest income is taxed as ordinary income.

If you are buying bonds for safety and to reduce portfolio volatility, you may want to look at a Fixed Indexed Annuity contract as an alternative because they are safer than bonds and historically have performed equal to or better than bonds. If you are thinking of buying bonds for income, be sure you can hold the bonds until maturity. Be careful with bond funds in a rising interest rate environment like we are in currently; that is the time to consider using an SPIA instead because it is a safer and more tax efficient way to generate the retirement income you need.

Chapter 4

GETTING YOUR LEGAL HOUSE IN ORDER

Most of my clients are not comfortable losing 30, 40, or 50 percent of their money in one year. Therefore, I have created systems that are designed to help my clients maximize their returns, minimize volatility, and find the safest way to generate inflation-adjusted income for life.

But what if you lost 30, 40, or 50 percent of your estate because you didn't have proper estate documents? Estate planning requires legal advice that will make sure your estate is going to be distributed the way you would like. If done properly, estate planning can greatly reduce the taxes required upon your death. My clients look to me to coach their financial lives. I don't give legal advice, but I do refer clients to two local estate planning attorneys who are very good at what they do: Richard Tizzano and John Kenney.

I've interviewed both Richard and John for this book and included their interviews below. I hope you might glean a little something from each of them. I have listed their contact information at the end of each interview as a resource for you and especially for those folks who reside right here in Kitsap County.

The purpose of each interview was to determine the basic estate documents everyone should have. In some cases, we also discussed a few of the lesser known and advanced estate planning concepts briefly.

A WORD OF CAUTION! Estate planning and the laws around this subject are unique to the state in which you live. Because most of the people I serve are here in Washington State, I focused on the issues in Washington State. Obviously if you are reading this outside of Washington State, you should consult with an expert estate planning attorney in your area.

INTERVIEW WITH JOHN KENNEY

JASON: John, what exactly is estate planning, why is it important, and what are some of the essential documents that everybody should have?

JOHN: Estate planning is a method whereby an individual, couple, or family can create a plan or a structure in order to prepare for an eventual or potential incapacity and inevitable death. The idea and the notion behind estate planning is that you want to make sure **you** decide what happens with yourself, your property, and/or your minor children, rather than having the State decide or the State laws decide. Good estate planning would be something that carries out your plans and wishes, as well as minimizes every tax or cost possible so your family is not unnecessarily burdened with those kinds of taxes and costs. A number of components make up proper estate planning.

JASON: One of the consequences of not having estate documents is you don't get to decide how your estate is going to be distributed; what happens then? You mentioned the State has a plan?

JOHN: Yes, the State has laws that decide how an individual's property will be divided and distributed if that person or married couple does not have an estate plan. For example, I recently had a prospective client whose husband had died without a will. So Dad died, Mom is still alive, and Dad has adult children from a prior relationship. The title of the real estate the husband and wife owned did not clearly state whether the wife had a "right of survivorship." Dad's adult children could potentially lodge a claim against the home that the husband thought was going to his wife when he died because he did not have a will. These examples come up all the time, but the State has a plan, and it is not always what the person, couple, or family desires.

JASON: Okay, I know there are different levels of estate planning depending on people's needs, but what are the basic documents that everyone should have regardless of the level of wealth he or she has?

JOHN: Sure. I will go through them and then I will circle back and explain why. At minimum, everyone should have a will and a financial power of attorney, also called a durable power of attorney. You should also have a healthcare power of attorney and a living will. Another document you'll need is a HIPAA authorization, which is now required by the Health Insurance Portability and Accountability Act.

A will basically does two primary things for a person: it divides your property according to your wishes, and if you have minor children, it will name guardians for those children. Without it, the State or courts will decide how your property is distributed and who will take care of your minor children if you, or your spouse, pass away.

The financial power of attorney, which is often called a durable power of attorney, gives someone else the power to make decisions for you if you become incapacitated and are unable to manage your own financial or legal affairs because of a legal condition, a health condition, or some other thing that is affecting your capacity to make decisions.

The document will assign an agent or attorney-in-fact to make those decisions for the individual who is incapacitated. Without it, the State will decide how your legal and financial affairs are going to be managed, and the State will appoint someone to do that for you.

Some people say, "Well, I don't care; let the State decide," but the process of letting the State decide can be very expensive for anyone you've left behind. Whereas, creating a will and/or durable power of attorney would allow your family to avoid that unnecessary expense and avoid allowing the state to take the control out of your hands.

JASON: Whom do people typically appoint as their financial power of attorney or their durable power of attorney?

JOHN: If it is a married couple and the other spouse is capable, the healthy spouse is usually appointed. I say healthy spouse because one will be unhealthy or incapacitated if the durable power of attorney has to come into play. Oftentimes, we will also have clients name a secondary person because it is possible that the spouse could either die or become incapacitated also. Clients will often appoint adult children if they have adult children who are responsible and they trust.

It is important that the individual be trustworthy and capable of managing someone's legal and financial affairs. If clients do not have adult children or spouses whom they trust or who are capable, they will name a trusted friend, and ultimately, if they do not have any friends who are capable or who they trust, they could name a professional such as a CPA, attorney, or financial advisor whom they trust or have trusted in their lives.

JASON: Why do they call it either financial or durable power of attorney?

JOHN: People use powers of attorney at various times throughout their lives. If you are buying a car, the dealer will actually give you what is called a limited power of attorney so the dealer can file your title and registration for you when you purchase that car. Anyone who has bought a car has probably signed one of these things. Limited purpose powers of attorney expire when the person's purpose is completed.

Often, you will give power of attorney to a spouse to accomplish certain tasks. Those are also limited and expire. If you become incapacitated, you don't want your power of attorney to expire, so a durable power of attorney will endure your incapacity and continue throughout it and not expire.

JASON: I want to back up just a minute. Will you speak for a minute about what probate is and how it works with a will?

JOHN: Absolutely. Basically there are four primary purposes of probate. Number one is, if an individual has a will, to take that will and read it, and ultimately, distribute the property or the assets to the individuals whom the will says to distribute them to and in the manner it states.

Secondarily, the purpose of probate is to notify any creditors of the death of this individual so the creditors can make a claim to get paid any money the deceased owed them. That is why you will often see in the newspapers long notices in the classified sections that will say "notice to creditors" of the probate of the deceased individual.

Third, as I mentioned before, is to appoint guardians for minor children if a person had minor children. The court actually appoints the guardian, but the will tells the court whom the deceased person wished to appoint.

The last purpose of a probate procedure is to notify all of the heirs or beneficiaries or people who want to claim to be an heir of the deceased. I often have clients who want to avoid probate so we will create a revocable living trust, which we can talk about later, because a revocable living trust avoids probate if created and implemented correctly.

I once had one client who told me he wanted to avoid probate because thirty years earlier he had had an illegitimate child, and he wanted to avoid the notice that goes out in the paper so this individual wouldn't come to the probate process and try to make a claim against the net worth of his estate and emotionally upset his spouse.

In some states, probate can be very expensive. Thankfully, in Washington State it is not that expensive relative to other states, such as California. One thing many people do not know about or are unaware of, is that if they own property in multiple states, then a probate is necessary in every state where they own property. Property is not necessarily only real estate. It can be a timeshare that has a contract. It can be an investment account that you opened when you were in college in California. I had one client who died, and unbeknownst to his children, he had opened an investment account in LA while he was in college. It had grown to a substantial amount, but he had never transferred it to a local branch; the State of California made the family go through probate in California because California is one of those very expensive states and the state wanted its piece of the action.

Probate in Washington State, without an aggravating-factor, like out-of-state property, is not that expensive and not that problematic. By law, the court is required to take four months. That is the absolute minimum that a probate process can take because it is written in the law.

Typically, a standard-type probate will take six to nine months and sometimes a year. I did a probate that lasted five years because the individual who died had some creditors who were trying to come after that individual at the time of his death, so it took five years to resolve all of those creditors' claims. All the children of this individual stood waiting until the claims were resolved, and then the children were eventually paid their inheritance.

JASON: I heard probate is a public process, and that concerns some people. What is it that concerns people about it being a public process?

JOHN: It can concern people because they do not want people who claim to be their creditors to come after their spouse or their children, or to try and take their property. Also, as I mentioned, they may not want their potential heirs or probably more accurately, the people who claim to be heirs, to try and make a claim against the net worth of their estate.

More importantly, the probate files and court records are also available to the public. My partner and I have found social security numbers on numerous occasions when we were looking back at old probate records and court files.

These files contain the address of your real estate, the value of your real estate, and sometimes, they contain your social security numbers. They should not, but it happens. Anybody can check out files and find that information at the court clerk's counter, and in some counties in Washington where the records are all online, you could actually go online and find it. For people who have a desire to be private, it is not the best alternative because it is all public.

JASON: Jumping forward, what is healthcare power of attorney, why is it important, and who should have it?

JOHN: A healthcare power of attorney is similar to a regular power of attorney because it becomes effective if someone is incapacitated. An individual pre-approves or pre-appoints another individual, usually called a healthcare agent, who is healthy and able to make decisions, to make healthcare choices for that individual.

The healthcare choices can be as simple as the individual needing some surgery, but he or she is unconscious and not able to authorize it for him or herself, so the healthcare agent just goes ahead and authorizes the surgery. Then that individual wakes up, and he or she is fine.

It could also be as serious and grave as making the decision to remove life support, which is one of the specific powers usually appointed to the healthcare agent. I tell people to choose someone who has his or her head on his shoulders as far as managing finances and legal things for his financial power of attorney, but being a healthcare agent takes more than that.

Sometimes healthcare decisions have spiritual consequences. Sometimes they have heavy emotional consequences so the individual you are choosing to be your healthcare agent should have the ability to make these types of emotional and spiritual life-ending decisions.

Oftentimes, when an individual goes in for routine surgeries, the hospital will ask whether the person has a living will and healthcare power of attorney. The living will is yet another document that expresses an individual's desire if he or she is in a specific condition such as permanently brain dead, comatose, or other permanently ill-type conditions. There are a number of definitions, but those are the most common.

An individual makes a decision in advance about whether to be kept alive, meaning the body's brain is dead and not functioning, but medical providers are keeping the body's blood and lungs pumping indefinitely with machinery and respirators, or not. Would that individual prefer to have life support removed so he or she can just pass away? The medical agent or healthcare agent who is appointed in the healthcare power of attorney would make that decision with the family members in counsel with the doctors.

The reason these two documents are very important is, first, keeping somebody alive in the hospital without the proper legal authorization to remove life support can be very, very emotional on a family, and if no one is appointed to make that decision, sometimes the decision is never made.

The second consequence is financial. People fail to realize in the immediate situation, until a month or two later, the financial consequences. For instance, if a husband and wife did not have a lot of savings, did not have a living will and/or a healthcare power of attorney, could not make the decision, and let the individual kind of linger for a week or two, then the medical bills can be tens of thousands of dollars per day. I have had clients who said, "Yeah, Mom had a living will, but we let her stay alive an extra three or four days to let the family fly in and gather, and it cost us an extra $100,000." People do not sometimes grasp the financial consequences you can leave your spouse with if, in fact, you do not have a document like this.

The final document, just to mention it briefly, that goes along with these other documents is the HIPAA authorization. Anybody who has ever been to a doctor in the last five or six years has signed something that has this acronym HIPAA on it.

In 2003, a federal law went into effect that says no individual is allowed to receive healthcare information about another individual without prior pre-authorization. This law made it illegal for medical providers to pass healthcare information to family members or healthcare agents without pre-authorization so the HIPAA authorization lists all these people and allows the medical providers to disclose that person's condition to them so they can make decisions regarding him or her. How can you make decisions if you can't be told what the condition is?

JASON: I have heard of people listing more than one executor on their wills to carry out their wishes. Is that a good idea?

JOHN: No. I try to counsel them out of it when they list joint executors or all three of their children as co-executors. I tell them of a horror story I once had with a client—an elderly woman who had emphysema. When she came to see me, she was probably going to die within a couple of years. She put down both of her children as co-executors. Up to that point, I had not had any personal experience with such cases, but the professors in law school always cautioned us about this kind of situation.

My client assured me that her children got along fine and were great friends. Within a couple of days of her death, both of her children called me and each one said the other was a drug addict and had been stealing from their mom for years and should not serve as an executor, but of course, the one speaking to me claimed to be capable and wanted to do it alone.

I was mom's attorney, so I withdrew from representing either of them. They then individually hired their own attorneys, and I was told by the attorneys that they spent about $10,000 sorting out who would be the personal representative. Sadly, that woman's estate was probably only worth about $60,000, so they drained about one-sixth of what they would have inherited just fighting over who would be personal representative. The personal representative only carries out a mechanical function. The person cannot give more money to him or herself. It was very unfortunate, but the lesson I learned is it can be problematic to have two executors because they always have to agree on everything. People are not always going to agree despite your thinking that they will do what is best.

JASON: When should people consider getting a revocable living trust and why would they want that in addition to having the basic documents?

JOHN: A lot of people think that having a revocable living trust is just for the wealthy, and to a certain extent, that is true. I do it for a lot of my higher net worth clients, but there is another reason that has nothing to do with your level of wealth: to avoid probate.

Probate is not a terrible process, but certain people want to avoid it entirely either because of the privacy issues, the time it takes, or the cost.

They may want to have the settlement of their estate be private, so with the revocable living trust, nothing is published in the newspaper. All the documents are kept with your attorney and family members. Nothing is given out, so the privacy factor is an important part of it.

Again, the probate process can take six to nine months on average, sometimes five years or longer. With a revocable trust, we can usually wrap up distributing property within thirty to forty-five days, unless there is real estate that has to be sold, which is dependent on the real estate market and not the laws.

The legal and attorney's fees for the distribution and wrapping up of the revocable living trust is usually going to be under $1,000, and probate, on average, in Kitsap County is about $3,000 to $5,000, so the cost savings that people can realize may be important to them.

On the other hand, a basic will is just that—very basic. It is not designed off-the-shelf to do a lot of things. Many of my clients have adult children who are married, and they don't just want their trustee or their executor to write a check to an adult child and say, "Here's your share." They want to protect that inheritance for their children from a child's potential divorce. When a parent sets up a trust and continues that trust for the benefit of a child or multiple children, that trust is in most cases exempt from divorce. It is also usually exempt from those children's creditors if they get into bad debt situations; it is exempt from creditors whom they may not know about; for instance, if they run somebody over in their car.

It is also exempt from bankruptcy court, so if they file bankruptcy as a result of bad creditor problems, that trust is exempt.

Likewise, using a revocable living trust can provide protection if you are concerned about your spouse remarrying someone who might take the money from that spouse. The spouse can be provided for and receive money from the trust, and the trust can specify that the spouse cannot change it or give it away to the new spouse.

I had a situation where I worked on a case about two years ago. In fact, it is still ongoing. An individual who was a dentist and had $3-4 million had been married for thirty or more years when his wife passed away. He had four adult children at the time. He remarried a few years after his wife's death. The joke among the four adult children was that his new wife was a mail order bride because she had just shown up from Eastern Europe one day and they were married.

This second marriage lasted five or six years before he died. After his death, his second wife revealed that he had created a new will after they were married and the new will disinherited all four of his adult children and left all of his wealth to her and her children. They are now suing her on the only grounds they have—that he was incapacitated, because he had Alzheimer's, when he executed the second will.

The children do not have much of a chance to overturn the will. If their mom or dad had created a will or a revocable living trust that had protected the children's inheritance, then none of this would have been an issue. But of course, he fell in love with his new mail order bride and her children whom she imported from Eastern Europe, so his first wife's children were left with nothing when there was plenty to go around.

Finally, as I mentioned earlier, if you have property out-of-state including a bank or investment account or time-shares, you are usually required to go through probate in that other state. The costs can add up quickly if you take the cost of probate in Washington at $3,000-$5,000 and you add the other states' probate costs because you have an investment account in California, and a winter place down in Arizona—pretty soon you are looking at $15,000-$20,000 worth of legal fees. A lot of my clients who have winter places down in Southern California or Arizona set up a revocable trust to avoid probate in those states.

These are the high level, very general benefits of using a revocable living trust, and it definitely has some advantages over a basic will, but it is not for everyone. Someone with a very modest net worth, who does not care about avoiding probate and does not have property in multiple states, is probably just fine with a regular basic will.

JASON: I know some people put off getting these estate documents done because they are intimidated by lawyers and because they hear horror stories of costs ranging from $200-$500 per hour. Can you give our readers a range of what they could expect if a single person comes in, and he or she just wants the bare bones basic estate documents he or she should have? I know everybody's situation is going to be different, but just give us the big picture idea of what might be expected.

JOHN: I don't know if your audience geographically is all here in Kitsap County, but basically in Kitsap County, for any capable and competent estate planning attorney, a basic will package, and I say the word "package" because it includes all the powers of attorney we talked about, the living will, as well as a HIPAA authorization, should range anywhere from $600-$1,000 total when there are no complexities in the individual's situation. For a married couple, it would be double that amount. If you go over to King County, the fee is probably going to be $900-$1,500 for the same basic will package just because those attorneys are paid a lot more and the firms charge a lot more over there. These figures are just a general range and will vary for each situation.

JASON: So it could be as little as $600 and up to maybe $5,000 if somebody has a very complex trust or has several different trusts that need to be created?

JOHN: Yes, and if you go to a revocable living trust, you can generally add at least $1,000 onto that base fee of the basic will package. Oftentimes, as you mentioned, someone may have multiple trusts, which will cost more, and I haven't even mentioned life insurance trusts. A life insurance trust, commonly called an ILIT for the acronym representing irrevocable life insurance trust, is often used to help avoid estate taxes on life insurance policies.

Estate taxes are the taxes the State of Washington and the federal government can charge an individual after that person is dead. Often, people don't realize that the life insurance proceeds come into play under the estate tax as well. They may have $300,000 or $400,000 net worth, but also have $1-2 million in life insurance policies. It is very important when we talk to clients to evaluate what they have as far as their current net worth, as well as their life insurance because a life insurance trust can avoid all estate taxes for that life insurance policy.

JASON: What is going on with federal and state estate taxes?

JOHN: Up until December 17, 2010, we were uncertain as to what would happen because the estate tax, as it was written back in 2001 and revised in 2003, was due to expire on December 31, 2010. Congress had gone back to the drawing board. The Republicans were fighting for an elimination of the estate tax. Democrats didn't want to eliminate the estate tax because, of course, they need to pay for the entire deficit. So they passed a law that is, in all of the estate planning community's opinion, just a band-aid. They passed a two-year fix on the estate tax that allows each individual to own up to $5 million of wealth, including life insurance, and be able to die without having to pay a federal estate tax. That amount per spouse allows a married couple a credit up to $10 million. However a certain amount of estate planning is required to insure that both spouses get their credit and that one credit is not lost on the first spouse's death. This is vital and can result in a lot of extra tax being owed if not done properly.

Now, a lot of my clients and a lot of individuals I work with here in Washington State were doing back flips and thinking, "Yay! I've got $3 million of net worth, and I don't have to pay estate tax on it." But a lot of the individuals in Washington don't realize that Washington has an estate tax and that Washington's estate tax does not match the federal one. Washington's estate tax credit is only $2 million, so anything above $2 million is subject to Washington

State's estate tax. Washington State's estate tax starts at 10 percent and tops out at 19 percent so for anything over the $2 million mark, you won't pay a federal tax if it's still under $5 million, but you could potentially pay a pretty high State of Washington tax. A married couple could avoid the Washington estate tax also but only with proper advance planning.

JASON: And what is the top rate for the federal estate tax if you have more than $5 million? Some of my clients may only have $2 million today, but they are only fifty years old, and if their money is compounding at 8 percent per year for the next thirty years—doubling every nine years—they could very easily end up with a sizeable estate.

JOHN: Right now, for the next two years, along with this $5 million credit, the top federal estate tax rate is 35 percent.

JASON: So potentially 50+ percent of your estate could go to paying estate taxes if you have a higher net worth between your federal estate taxes and taxes here in Washington State?

JOHN: Correct.

JASON: John, is there anything else you would like to add that you think would be relevant to the readers with respect to estate planning, basic documents, or other concerns people should be thinking about?

JOHN: As you mentioned earlier, a lot of people don't like talking to attorneys, but the good estate planning attorneys will try to make the experience proactive for the client. They want the client to participate in the process rather than just being told this is how they're going to do it. I have had clients complain that attorneys will just write something up, not explain it very well, and then just have them sign it.

Good attorneys will ask a lot of questions and usually charge a flat fee. The beauty of a flat fee is that clients don't have to fear the cost of the unknown fees. The unknown total of a project with an hourly charge of $150-$200 is scary. I charge a flat fee which means this is the analysis I have gone through, and for me to do the work we are proposing, it is going to be X dollars and no more. It provides a lot of certainty and can eliminate a lot of those fears.

Then the final thing I would mention is because we only have a two-year window with this current law, it is important now more than ever that individuals get in to see a capable and competent estate planning attorney so they can discuss their estate planning needs. Beyond 2012, we still don't know what will happen, so you have to have an estate plan that is designed and implemented to give you the maximum flexibility for whatever the estate tax laws will be.

The good estate planning attorneys will have documents and software that will create the maximum flexibility for your estate planning needs given the current laws. Be careful of attorneys who are one day a divorce attorney, the next a personal injury attorney, and then the next day your estate attorney. They are not always going to be on the cutting edge with all of their estate planning documents needed for designing a plan with the most flexibility.

JASON: That brings up a good question. You open up the phone book, you turn to "A" in the yellow pages, and there are ninety pages of attorneys listed. How do people know whether they are working with a good estate planning attorney? How can they help narrow that search, or what are some resources they could consider?

JOHN: Well, there are national organizations that give designations to estate planning attorneys. One of them is called American College of Trust and Estate Planning Counsel. I do not believe we have any ACTEPC estate planning attorneys here in Kitsap County; almost all of them are in Seattle. You should also choose one that has a narrower niche or only practices estate planning. For example, I practice business law, tax law, and estate planning. All three have to do with tax laws so my focus is pretty narrow and specific to those areas.

One thing that differentiates me from some of my colleagues here in Kitsap County is that I have what is called an LLM, which is a master's degree in tax law. That means I was sick enough to go back to law school for two more years beyond the regular three-year law degree to get more advanced training and education just in tax and estate planning, so look for that and any other designations the attorney may have. But the most important thing, especially in a community such as Kitsap County, is to ask whether the person's primary area of focus is estate planning. In Kitsap County, you see a lot of generalist attorneys who do a little bit of everything, which means they may not be very good at any one thing, and that can be dangerous and costly when it comes to estate planning.

JASON: All right. Thank you, sir.

Luce, Lineberry & Kenney ps
Attorneys at Law
John Kenney, LLM
17791 Fjord Dr NE Suite 154
Poulsbo, WA 98370-8482
(360) 850-1049
john@lklawgroup.com

INTERVIEW WITH RICHARD TIZZANO

JASON: Richard, I was hoping you could start out with helping me understand what exactly is estate planning?

RICHARD: I like to say estate planning is different from financial planning; financial planning folks help you grow your money, and good estate planning can help you distribute your money in a most effective manner to the people and the charities you want to see blessed, and perhaps even give you a strategy for how to do that while you're alive, as well as after you've died.

JASON: What are some of the essential documents everybody should have when developing an estate plan?

RICHARD: Everyone should have a power of attorney for financial matters, a power of attorney for medical matters, a living will, which in Washington is called a directive to physicians, and a will. Then it might be appropriate for some folks to have a living trust, special needs trust, or life insurance trust, or some other more advanced-type estate planning documents.

JASON: I would like to get some clarification on what each one of these documents is and what its purpose is. So what exactly is the power of attorney for financial matters, and why does somebody need it?

RICHARD: You would be authorizing someone to assist you with financial matters. It does not limit or take away your ability to control and manage your own finances, but it allows someone else to participate. That can be done in a few different ways. You can have someone not be appointed until some event happens where you become incapacitated, and in that scenario, the authority would be springing into effect when you were deemed to be incapacitated, either you had some accident or at some point your dementia is at a level where the doctor is willing to say, "No, you're not able to manage your own affairs."

Or it can be effective immediately when you sign the document. I recommend people consider that first, because it makes it much easier for a person to receive help from the person he or she trusts. The document doesn't have to be given out immediately when the person signs it, but the person has it, and if something unforeseen happens, then the person named, who is aware he or she has been named, can come and get the document and act on the person's behalf.

The more typical scenario is where someone begins to become more frail or have a bad day or whatever and needs somebody to take care of something, and if the document is effective immediately when it was signed, the person needing help can just give the other person the document and ask him or her to go take care of the matter with the financial institution. The same goes with a power of attorney for medical. The person can go talk to the doctor or access records immediately. The person does not have to have a determination of incapacity just to effectuate the document.

JASON: Who do people usually list as their power of attorney?

RICHARD: They usually list their spouses first and then a child they may trust or a child who may have a specific ability as an accountant or physician or something, and then after that, it is friends or neighbors.

JASON: Do you have a specific example of a time when somebody had a power of attorney and it really helped him, or a time when somebody probably should have had a power of attorney, and it really handicapped him because he didn't have that type of document?

RICHARD: I can combine it into one story that will make you aware of the shortcomings of a power of attorney. A son came in whose his dad was failing. He felt like his dad really needed to be in a nursing home, but his dad didn't want to go. The son had power of attorney for his father, and said as much to his dad, thinking he could force his dad to go. His dad got angry and said, "Well, I'm revoking the power of attorney."

That is one of the aspects of a power of attorney; unless it is agreed to by all parties or opposed by the court, it's revocable at any time. I tell people when they sign it, if the agent or attorney-in-fact doesn't do what you want him to do, you can always fire him. So the dad fired the son, and the son felt powerless and said, "Well, I'd like to get a guardianship of my dad."

I explained to him that even if he were named as the guardian for his dad, he wouldn't have the authority to force his dad to do what he doesn't want to do. He would, however, have the authority to control his father's checkbook and his finances, and the court action would cut off his father's ability to access his own finances.

In Washington, we have what's called "the right to rot," which gives his dad the ability to decide what kind of care he wants or doesn't want. Even if the court deems him to be incompetent, you can't impose a level of care on him that he doesn't want unless there is an imminent danger to him or others, and that is a pretty high standard. If he doesn't want to take his medication, doesn't want to go to the nursing home, and wants to sit in front of the TV and eat bonbons and drink beer, he can do whatever he wants to do.

Having to have guardianship is a consequence of not having a power of attorney, but having a guardianship does not necessarily solve all the problems that come along with it. So, if someone does not have a power of attorney, whether it is for medical or healthcare, and he or she gets to the place where he is not able to care for himself, a guardianship has to be appointed.

I get people who come in occasionally and say, "Well I noticed my neighbor isn't taking the garbage out, and the mail is piling up in the mailbox. I went and visited him, and he seemed to be okay, but something's just not right." So we try to find out where the person's kids are or who the person is connected to. Sometimes there's nobody around, and it's either the neighbor, or the sister-in-law in Arizona trying to figure out how she's going to manage as the guardian for her sister-in-law up here who has to find someone locally who can assist her in that guardianship.

If you are one of those people now in need, but you don't have any powers of attorney because there was really nobody who was close enough to you that you wanted to select, or you just didn't know you needed a power of attorney, and then you get to the place where you need help, without those simple documents, it is going to require a guardianship before the court. The court will have to make a determination whether you are or you're not competent to manage your own affairs. If you're not, then the court will choose the most logical person who can step in and do that on your behalf, and if there is no obvious person like a relative or close friend, then it will assign a professional guardian who would have to step in at that point and fill that role.

JASON: So, if you don't take it upon yourself to have these documents in good order before they are needed, then the court has to get involved in determining who it thinks would be the best person for filling that role? Most people probably don't want the court making that decision for them I would imagine.

RICHARD: Well, I would agree, most people don't, but it's sad that a lot of people don't have an option. They don't go to church, or there's nobody in the church they've gotten close to, or all the people they have been close friends with have died. They have other peers, but they were never really close to those people, and their kids are far away, or they don't have kids, so they don't really have an option. It's not just a matter of realizing that, "Gee, I should name somebody," and having the inertia to get it done. Sometimes it's beyond that. I've had people come in and they want to get it done, but when I ask the question, "Who would you name?" I get a blank stare. They just realize there is nobody in their lives they can trust to do that, and they think that maybe I have an accountant I could trust for the financial part, so sometimes it gets really difficult.

JASON: So the medical power of attorney is different from the financial. The financial is going to give that person the ability to act on his or her behalf on financial matters, but what does the medical power of attorney give someone? How much authority, if somebody has a medical power of attorney, does that person have? Does the person just have the ability to access doctor's records or does he or she have the ability to make medical decisions for people?

RICHARD: Well again, you're authorizing someone to act on your behalf, but it does not take away your ability to act on your own behalf. I used to have a medical power of attorney that would be effective when you became incompetent, but again, I think this is a situation where the document is most effective if it's effective immediately because with the new health privacy act, the doctors are reluctant even to give medical information to your spouse.

If you have a power of attorney for healthcare that is effective immediately and your spouse wants to call the doctor, or if you're named on there for your parent and you want to call the doctor, you can fax it over to the doctor and say it's effective immediately. The doctor can then say, "Yeah, I did see your mom last week and this is what happened," or "These are the drugs I prescribed," or "This is the problem." If you decide, "Well, Mom, you need a second opinion," you can call the office, arrange to have the records sent, and if the power of attorney is effective immediately, that allows you to do that, but again, if your mom says, "No, I don't want you to meddle; I'm going to revoke the power of attorney," she could always do that because she still maintains that control.

JASON: What is the living will and why is that important?

RICHARD: The living will or directive to physicians is important because it is addressing a situation where you are no longer able to tell the medical community what kind of care you want, so either your dementia has gotten so bad you can't communicate, or you're highly medicated, you have a head injury, you have some kind of terminal illness, death is imminent, or you can't communicate, so the person you've named in your power of attorney for your healthcare has the authority to assert this other document, this directive to physicians or this living will, on your behalf to address the kind of care you would want now that you're at the end of your life.

So you can't tell them at that point, "Because I'm dying and I can't eat, I do not want a feeding tube," but this document addresses those issues. Your status as attorney-in-fact, under the power of attorney, asserts that power and can tell the doctor that when the person was competent he said if death were imminent, he didn't want a feeding tube, he did not want hydration, or he did not want pain medication. It says here if his heart stops under these circumstances, he does not want CPR. It can address all those end-of-life issues.

I explain to people we can put whatever they want in there. One client said, "Well, I want you to put down that when I die, I'm buried with a cell phone, a candy bar, and a flashlight." I said we can do that, and then she laughed and said she was only kidding, but I have some people who are Jehovah's Witnesses, so they can't take a blood transfusion, and they want that in the directive to the physicians. They do not want that kind of care. My partner had a female client who said if they pass a piece of Hawaiian pizza under her nose three times and there's no reaction, then they can go ahead and disconnect her.

JASON: What about a will? Why is a will important, who should have one, and what does a will do?

RICHARD: A will directs whom you want to manage your estate after your death, so it allows for the appointment of an executor. The executor has some duties by law to open the probate, to advertise your death to the creditors, to consolidate or marshal all the aspects, to pay any taxes if there are any, and to assess and pay any creditors' claims if they're valid, and then to distribute what's remaining to all of the named beneficiaries as you have described in your will.

The misconception a lot of people have is now that they have a will, their kids can avoid probate, but a will doesn't avoid probate. The will is the document that is used in the probate process to appoint the people you want appointed and to direct how you want things distributed.

JASON: I know when meeting with your clients that probate is a concern for them. What exactly is probate? I know it is a public process. What can you tell us about it, and why might people be hesitant to go through probate? How much time does it take?

RICHARD: I'm licensed in California and in the state of Washington and the process is pretty different in both states in the sense that California is much more detailed, much more involved, and the court is much more a part of the process, and therefore, I would say it is approximately ten times more expensive to do a probate in the state of California than in the state of Washington. So in California, people have a real sense of urgency to avoid the probate process, and that is where the living trust idea is effective. In Washington, the process is not nearly as onerous, and it is not nearly as expensive.

JASON: Is it likely to change or is it likely to stay as simple and as clean as it is now?

RICHARD: I don't see any move in the legislature toward change. There is legislation coming along in the area of protecting vulnerable adults, but nothing that I can see impacting probate. I think the public is satisfied for the most part with that probate process.

JASON: So, in the state of Washington, because it is a simpler, cleaner process, and less expensive maybe than California, how long would you say the average probate takes to have somebody's estate distributed according to the will?

RICHARD: An estate that does not include real estate would probably on average take nine months. There is a statutory requirement that the probate has to be open at least four months to allow for creditors' claims. The person dies and it takes a few weeks to get to the attorney, and then it takes a couple of weeks to get it open with the court. Then once the executor is appointed and the notice to creditors is published in the paper, the four-month period starts, so by the end of the four months, you are already six months down the line.

Once the creditors' claim period is over, then the executor is free to distribute assets because no creditor claims can be accepted after that period of time. The executor is free to distribute it without worrying that some creditor is going to show up and want to be paid. Then the receipts from the beneficiaries are filed and probate can be closed.

JASON: One of the concerns I have heard people express is that probate is a public process. Why would that be a concern to people?

RICHARD: Well, I got a book from a friend one Christmas called *Wills of the Rich and Famous*. All this author had done was get copies of famous people's wills from the court files by going around to the different jurisdictions where these famous people had died and where their wills were probated. He put them all together and made a book out of it. I think Jackie Kennedy was in there, John Kennedy, Frank Sinatra, and a couple of baseball players, so it was interesting.

A lot of it was just legalese, but I kind of cut to the dicey parts about whom they were leaving stuff to and how they were trying to avoid taxes or whatever. Some people are very private, and they are uncomfortable with the idea that anybody, even the black sheep of the family whom they don't want to know their business, can just go down to the courthouse and ask for the file and be allowed to look at it and see who got what. There's an inventory that's usually filed with the court so people can see everything you had and who got it.

JASON: Does a living trust come into play for people who don't want a nine-month process with probate or want a more private closing of their affairs?

RICHARD: Yes.

JASON: So, before we talk about the living trust, I just want to recap; for the bare minimum that everyone should have, the four documents are: the power of attorney for financial matters, the power of attorney for medical matters, a living will, and a will. Is that correct?

RICHARD: Yes.

JASON: So tell us a little bit more about living trusts. Who would want a living trust, and why might he or she want the living trust?

RICHARD: Okay. Let me touch on the issue of the probate with real property because sometimes, in the market we have now, real property is going to be a problem.

JASON: What do you mean by real property?

RICHARD: Houses or anything that is connected with land. Some people might own their house or a rental or a resort place or a condo. That is an asset that may be hard to distribute if you have three kids and want to divide your estate equally between them.

If you have $300,000 in the bank, each kid gets $100,000 and you're done. If there is the house Mom and Dad have lived in for years, and then there's the little rental they have up the street, and $75,000 in the bank, it is more problematic in distributing that to the three kids. Decisions have to be made. Are the kids going to co-own the house, or put the house up for sale? When it comes to cleaning up the house, who is going to do it? All of those things take a lot of time to process through, so what may not seem like a quick nine months is a pretty quick time to get that all taken care of when it's just cash in the estate, but when you have these other assets in the estate, that time can really drag on.

I have seen where you have a couple of the kids think they can't sell the place, and they want to keep it and visit it every summer, so they may hang onto it for a year or two, but then they realize how expensive it is and how impractical it is, and finally after a couple of years, they've come to the conclusion that they need to sell it. Sometimes the estate stays open while that happens; sometimes they transfer it so just the siblings all own that property jointly. Real property is often a fly in the ointment as far as trying to distribute it efficiently or to close a probate.

Now that kind of issue is often the same, even if the assets are passing through a living trust versus a probate. So the way it works with a living trust is a twin of you is created; so it's not a separate entity in that it has a separate tax ID number, but it's a separate entity exactly like yourself. It has your own social security number. So this entity, which is not John Smith, but is the John Smith Trust, is created. It has John Smith's social security number, and John Smith is the trustee of it, and all the assets are controlled by John Smith Trustee. This legal fiction of sorts exists, and when John Smith the person dies, the John Smith Trust continues and then Mary Smith, who's named as the successor trustee, steps into John's shoes, and then Mary has the authority, as trustee, the same authority that John had to administer those assets, to manage them, to sell them if need be.

The trust directs that, when John dies, the three kids get what they're going to get, and then Mary has the authority to do whatever needs to be done to see that happens, pay the creditors if there are any, pay off other bills there may be, and consolidate the assets and distribute them to the beneficiaries. Mary can do all of that without court intervention because the trust owns the assets or controls the assets because they were titled in John Smith's name as trustee.

Usually, when a trust is created, a will is also created, and that will is called a pour-over will. It's a pour-over will by definition because the beneficiary of a pour-over will is the trust, so any particular asset that may show up that for some reason was not titled in John Smith's name may have to be probated, and then it pours over to the trust and is distributed according to the terms of the trust.

For example: John buys a winning lotto ticket, and then when he realizes it's the winning lotto ticket and he is going to get a million dollars a year for the next twenty years, he's so excited he dies of a heart attack. So John owns this asset; it's his, but it's not in his trust. There is no provision for the lotto people to pay the trust. It's John's ticket, and he went down to claim it just before he died, but again it's not in his trust, so what happens to that string of payments? Well, it has to go through probate.

The ticket is something John owned. He did not own it as trustee in his trust. He owned it individually, so there would be a probate of that particular asset and the beneficiary in the will is going to be the trust, so that pours into the trust, and then the new trustee in the trust would include the lottery winnings as the assets of the trust to be distributed with the other assets.

JASON: Okay. So if you have a living trust, then a pour-over will is an additional document you would have to make sure anything not titled will end up in the trust and be distributed the way you want. I have heard you should consider a trust in Washington State if you own real property outside of the state. Why might that be?

RICHARD: That is one of the questions I ask folks when they want some advice on getting a trust. I ask them, "Do you want to avoid probate?" Some people have had a good experience with probate, and they don't care, but for some people, for whatever reason, the probate has been a nightmare and they will say, "I absolutely don't want my kids to have to go through probate."

I ask them, "Do you have a taxable estate?" and we can talk about that in a minute, and "Do you own property in states other than Washington State?" Having a trust allows you to avoid probate, not only in Washington, but you can avoid probate in any other state in which you own real property. Otherwise, there has to be a probate.

It's called an ancillary probate when it's not for a state where you are a resident. If you own property in that state, a probate needs to be done to transfer that property to wherever you want to transfer it, if it's not held in your trust. So when I have clients who own property in a few states, I tell them, "It's a no-brainer; you need to have a trust."

JASON: What is the proper term when somebody is a trustee who takes over?

RICHARD: Successor trustee.

JASON: Is it a good idea to have more than one executor or more than one successor trustee, or can that cause problems?

RICHARD: It depends on whether the person you named is able to do it by him or herself, and whether he or she will do a good job or not. I have had some people who have kids who have fought like cats and dogs their whole lives, but they think, "When I die, it will bring my kids together. If I name them as co-trustees, they will be able to start this new relationship."

That's a mistake. You need to name someone you trust and who can at least balance a checkbook. The person must like to pay attention to detail and appear to be responsible in the financial area. The person is not a procrastinator. That is the kind of person you would want to be your trustee, and I have seen it where co-trustees have worked very well. It is a little more cumbersome because there are a number of situations where both people have to sign off on certain activities, and it may take a little more time or effort to get a few basic things done, but I think if the people get along, it can be helpful to have co-trustees. But if they don't get along, then there will be hell to pay.

JASON: Just a moment ago you mentioned a taxable estate. Would you speak to that for a moment?

RICHARD: Sure. There is a federal estate tax and a Washington State estate tax. That tax amount has changed over the course of time at both the state dollar amount and the federal dollar amount.

When a person dies, if he or she has a surviving spouse, the assets are able to pass to the surviving spouse without any state or federal estate tax because there is an unlimited marital deduction. Bill Gates could die and his surviving spouse would have no estate tax to pay, but when an individual dies or the surviving spouse dies, then all of their assets are added together.

That would include life insurance, retirement accounts, real property, toys, vehicles, boats, investment accounts, and timeshares. Everything you own is added up together, and if that total exceeds the amount that is allowed for you to pass on without imposing the estate tax, then it passes the state tax-free. But if it exceeds that number, then your estate is subject to paying that tax and the estate pays the tax, not the beneficiaries.

You can do a few things to reduce having to pay that tax, and they basically come down to reducing the size of your estate or the total value of your estate when you die. You could take advantage of the annual gift tax exemption. This year it is $13,000. It is ratcheted for inflation, so it may rise as time goes on, but it allows you to give money away to individuals at $13,000 a year to as many individuals as you wish.

If you have a lot of family, friends, and relatives, you could give each of those people $13,000. You could give your attorney $13,000, and your investment advisor $13,000, whoever you want. You can whittle away at your estate pretty quickly using the annual exclusion, and there is the unlimited marital exemption we talked about, so money could go to your spouse, but that would ultimately be subjected to tax.

You could give money to charity. If you give it to charity while you're alive, you get an income tax reduction. If you wait until you die, any money you give to charity at that point is deducted to your taxable estate and would go to charity, so you wouldn't have to pay any estate task on that amount, but your estate does not get an income tax deduction for the contribution to charity at your death.

JASON: Let me just run a quick example by you. Right now, today, and I know this is a moving target, so these numbers are going to change, but let's say there is a husband and wife. The husband dies. He ends up leaving everything to the wife, and now the wife has an estate of $10 million and she dies. So the couple had a total estate of $10 million. Are they looking at an estate tax with a $10 million estate? And if so, what would be the tax rate at the federal government approximately, and what would the state estate tax be? And I know this is probably some complex tax planning, but I'm just trying to get an idea for our readers what the consequences could be for people.

RICHARD: Okay. Well, the Washington State estate tax is on any assets above $2 million and the federal estate tax is on assets above

$5 million. Both of those exemptions are subject to the marital deduction. If you die, and you have just a simple "I love you will" and you want to pass everything to your spouse, that passes to the surviving spouse and is not subject to that tax, so taxes do not have to be paid after the death of the first spouse.

JASON: So when the husband dies, the wife gets all $10 million, and she does not owe any estate tax at that point?

RICHARD: Correct.

JASON: Now she dies. She has $10 million. How much would her estate tax be after those $5 million? Do you know what the current federal estate tax is?

RICHARD: It is 35 percent above the $5 million.

JASON: And the Washington State estate tax for amounts above the $2 million, any idea what that is?

RICHARD: So the $8 million, which is the amount above the $2 million, would be subject to the Washington State tax. Washington State tax is a graduated tax that starts at 10 percent and goes to 17 or 18 percent.

JASON: So worst case scenario for a higher net worth person is that almost 50 percent of his or her estate could be lost to taxes above those exclusion amounts without some proper planning.

RICHARD: Correct. So if this couple had a living trust, they could have provided for a credit trust to hold $2 million of the $5 million that belonged to the first spouse who died. That would have set aside that amount under the exemption of the first spouse, and the surviving spouse would have gotten all the income from that, and then the additional $3 million that belonged to them—we will just assume it was the community property interest of the decedent—that could be held in a qualified terminal interest property trust or a QTIP trust, which the Washington State tax would not have to be paid on until the surviving spouse died.

JASON: So if someone has an estate that is worth $5-$10 million, they should consult with an estate planner one-on-one because their needs will be more specific.

Or if they are around fifty years old and have an estate that is about $2.5 million dollars now, they should also meet with an estate planner because they should assume that their money, if it is earning 8 percent, over the next thirty years will double every nine years. This will quickly put them above the state and federal exclusions, so some planning may need to happen so they don't run into any estate tax problems in the future.

RICHARD: An interesting part of that $5 million, though, is if one spouse doesn't use it all, what was not used can shift over to the other spouse. So if the first spouse dies and he or she had an estate of $8 million, and the first spouse sheltered $4 million in their trust and then the surviving spouse's assets grew to $6 million dollars, the second spouse to die would have this $5 million, and the $1 million, which the first spouse didn't use, can be used by the other spouse.

JASON: Could you maybe touch briefly on when an irrevocable life insurance trust or a special needs trust might be needed, and who should be setting those up?

RICHARD: If you have a loved one who has a special need such as a disabled child, or maybe you want to remember your parent in your documents, whether it's your will or your trust, you can name that person as a beneficiary, but you must state that the share the person gets should be held in a special needs trust for the person's benefit.

So you would name somebody who would be the trustee of that trust for his or her benefit, and by doing it that way, rather than giving the person the money outright, you allow for a pool of money to be reserved to assist that person without interfering with the state or federal aid he or she may be getting.

So if you have a parent who is on Medicaid in a nursing home and you left him or her $50,000, he or she is going to be suddenly ineligible for Medicaid. If you left it to your parent in a special needs trust, then the trustee could use that money to provide extra care for your parent or get him or her an electric wheelchair or a van or something that Medicaid isn't going to pay for and the pool of money doesn't disqualify your parent from being eligible to continue to receive that Medicaid. The same would be true for a child who might be receiving assistance.

JASON: I see this concern come up a lot with parents of special needs children. They are worried their children will be cut off from some of these resources because of a lump-sum inheritance so a special needs trust would take care of that. What about the irrevocable life insurance trust? Who needs it, when does it come into play, and why do people look at those?

RICHARD: Most of the time as people age, they decide they don't need life insurance anymore. They don't have little kids at home, and they have a different pool of money. But an irrevocable life insurance trust might be helpful, especially a second-to-die policy which moves funds out of your estate into this trust.

If it is an irrevocable life insurance trust, it is not part of your estate when you die for estate tax purposes. You could cover possible taxes that may have to be paid at your death, pay off mortgages, or other things you think need to be taken care of when you die. You might be concerned about whether or not there's going to be liquid cash available in your estate to cover those kinds of things.

JASON: This would be especially important for people who have a lot of their wealth tied up in real estate since the federal government requires that the inheritance tax/estate tax be paid within a certain period of time, and cashing in the real property could take too long for you to pay the taxes on time. This creates a pool of money the beneficiaries could use for that.

RICHARD: It could be used to cover that or even a family business that has been inherited so it wouldn't have to be sold. It is a good way to generate the cash to pay possible taxes.

JASON: Some people put off getting even their basic estate planning documents created because they hear that attorneys charge $200, $300, or $400 per hour. What is a fair amount they should probably expect to pay to get those estate documents completed?

RICHARD: Well, it certainly depends on where your local attorney lives or practices, and it is a function of the time it takes the attorney to create the documents. But when you look at it in relation to some of the advertisements you hear that say, "Send in $29 and you can get this program that will give you a will for your estate and powers of attorney and you need to do it now," there really is a sense that what people are doing is basic, but there are also just some very key questions that need to be addressed that make it complicated, where it is just worth having assistance from that person who has been down the trail before you and can guide you along the way.

For instance, a simple will is pretty basic. You're going to name your executor and whom you want to get your assets, but as I referred to earlier, let's say you want to leave something to your mom or you have a disabled child; just being able to have that special needs trust provision in your document is going to make sure that what you want accomplished gets accomplished.

I have people who are older, and it's the same kind of thing with them. People have been married for years so they want to name each other. They don't want to name the kids, even if it means preserving some assets, so they can have a special needs provision for their spouse that says when I die, my half of the community property is held for the benefit of my spouse in a special needs trust. If the person dies and then the surviving spouse ends up going into a nursing home, that's half the estate that's salvaged from or not available for many key purposes.

JASON: I tell my clients there is a time to try to cut costs, and there's a time to make sure you're doing things right. The concern I have is if you do them wrong, you could end up costing yourself a lot more money in the long run, so you don't want to be pennywise and a pound foolish as the saying goes. But what would the possible range be for the basic package?

RICHARD: Sure, I was just kind of confirming that there is some value there. I think for a single person to get all of the documents we talked about—the powers of attorney, the directive to physicians, and the basic will—it will cost a minimum of about $400-$500. It will take a minimum of two meetings with your attorney plus the creation of the actual documents, which easily brings the total time for the attorney to a minimum of four hours. If we are talking about a couple, you might expect to pay $700-$750 to get all those documents done for both people.

If you're talking about a trust, you have the documentation on the trust, and then I generally recommend the attorney also handle transferring all the assets into the trust so it is done properly. If you don't transfer the assets to your trust properly, then you end up having to go through the whole probate as if you hadn't created a trust. There is a lot more work in the trust preparation, but for a single person, I think you would expect to pay $1,000-$1,200 minimum, and probably $1,600 or so for a couple.

JASON: So for a range of costs, we are talking anywhere from $400-$5,000 depending on how complex the estate is.

RICHARD: Sure. I think that is very well put.

JASON: Thank you, Richard. I appreciate your time here.

Sherrard, McGonagle, Tizzano
Attorneys at Law, Est. 1954
Richard C. Tizzano, PS
19717 Front Street
PO Box 400
Poulsbo, WA 98370
(360) 697-7132
richardt@legalpeaceofmind.com

Chapter 5

TAX PLANNING

The hardest thing in the world to understand is the income tax.
— Albert Einstein

When Mr. Jones came to see me, he and his wife were both sixty-five years old and enjoying their retirement. They were living comfortably on their retirement income, which was made up of both pensions and social security benefits. Mr. Jones had $500,000 dollars in his IRA, which he had no intention of ever using.

The primary purpose of the money was twofold: First, and foremost, if anything happened to Mr. Jones, he knew his wife would need the money to supplement her income because his pension would only pay her 55 percent; second, the purpose of the money was to leave it to his children.

Now Mr. Jones didn't realize when he turned seventy-and-a-half that the IRS was going to require him to start taking distributions from his IRA, the Required Minimum Distribution (RMD). Even though he didn't need the money, he was going to be required to pull money out.

Please note that the IRS can penalize up to 50 percent of your RMD if you don't take it every year. For example, if the IRS required you to take $40,000 dollars out of your retirement account the first year and you didn't, then it could impose a $20,000 penalty for that year.

So I asked Mr. Jones whether he had ever sat down to look at what the future tax liability might be on that IRA. We made some pretty conservative assumptions:

- Currently age sixty-five

- Assumed a 6 percent return annually on his investments

- He will take out his RMD every year and no extra

- Because of his family history and current health, we assume a life expectancy of age ninety.

PROJECTED IRA DISTRIBUTIONS

Year	Age Beg	Age End	Beginning Balance	6.00% Earnings	RMD Divisor	Required Distribution	Ending Balance
2009	64	65	$500,000	$30,000		$0	$530,000
2010	65	66	$530,000	$31,800		$0	$561,800
2011	66	67	$561,800	$33,708		$0	$595,508
2012	67	68	$595,508	$35,730		$0	$631,238
2013	68	69	$631,238	$37,874		$0	$669,113
2014	69	70	$669,113	$40,147	27.4	$24,420	$684,839
2015	70	71	$684,839	$41,090	26.5	$25,843	$700,087
2016	71	72	$700,087	$42,005	25.6	$27,347	$714,745
2017	72	73	$714,745	$42,885	24.7	$28,937	$728,692
2018	73	74	$728,692	$43,722	23.8	$30,617	$741,797
2019	74	75	$741,797	$44,508	22.9	$32,393	$753,912
2020	75	76	$753,912	$45,235	22.0	$34,269	$764,878
2021	76	77	$764,878	$45,893	21.2	$36,079	$774,691
2022	77	78	$774,691	$46,481	20.3	$38,162	$783,010
2023	78	79	$783,010	$46,981	19.5	$40,154	$789,837
2024	79	80	$789,837	$47,390	18.7	$42,237	$794,990
2025	80	81	$794,990	$47,699	17.9	$44,413	$798,276
2026	81	82	$798,276	$47,897	17.1	$46,683	$799,490
2027	82	83	$799,490	$47,969	16.3	$49,048	$798,411
2028	83	84	$798,411	$47,905	15.5	$51,510	$794,805
2029	84	85	$794,805	$47,688	14.8	$53,703	$788,790
2030	85	86	$788,790	$47,327	14.1	$55,943	$780,175
2031	86	87	$780,175	$46,811	13.4	$58,222	$768,764
2032	87	88	$768,764	$46,126	12.7	$60,533	$754,357
2033	88	89	$754,357	$45,261	12.0	$62,863	$736,755
2034	89	90	$736,755	$44,205	11.4	$64,628	$716,333

Total RMDs: $908,005

Total Taxed: **$1,624,338**

Hypothetical only - no specific investment illustrated.

Mr. Jones, over his life expectancy, could end up taking $900,000 dollars out of his IRA in RMDs. Remember, he doesn't want to take anything out, but he is required to by the IRS. When he dies, his IRA will still have $700,000 in it.

Now, assuming the worst case scenario, all of the money at this point transfers to his named beneficiary who chooses to take a lump sum distribution instead of stretching it out over his lifetime; then he would have total taxable distributions of $1.6 million.

Think about that for a minute. Today, Mr. Jones starts with $500,000, and upon his death, he will end up with $1.6 million of taxable distributions from his account.

We currently have some of the lowest marginal income tax rates in our country's history. So let's pretend that taxes aren't going to go up and we will be able to maintain these ultra low tax rates for the next twenty-five years. It seems a bit ridiculous to me to make this assumption given the amount of spending our government is doing, but let's pretend the tax rates will stay low to keep the math easy. If we assume Mr. Jones pays 25 percent tax on his $1.6 million of taxable distribution, he would be looking at a prolonged and future tax liability of $400,000.

Now if I were a betting man, I'd have to bet that taxes are going to go up in the future. Our national debt just hit $14 trillion and our government just created a socialized medicine plan, social security is on a pace to go belly up, and Medicare costs are skyrocketing. How in the world are we going to pay for all this unless taxes go up?

The question every person in our country should be asking is: "If I could protect my retirement account from excessive taxation, would I want to? Is there a better way?"

Maybe. It depends on how you plan to use your money and what's most important to you. But if you want to give Uncle Sam as little of your hard-earned money as possible, wouldn't you want to know how to do it?

Has your advisor talked to you about protecting your retirement from excessive taxation? If you have a retirement account and work with an advisor who is doing his job, then you should have some idea of what your future tax liability is.

Depending on how we choose to fix this problem, we can reduce that tax liability by up to 50 percent. Not only can we reduce a person's tax liability, but we can also structure his accounts so when he turns seventy-and-a-half, he won't be required to take any money out.

This structuring gives a person the ability to allow that account to compound and grow income tax free for decades. Imagine, tax free not just for his life, but also for the income his wife may need, and, if done properly, it could mean a lifetime of tax free distributions to his children for years and years and years. I don't know of anyone who wants to pay Uncle Sam more than he should, but how many of you would know whether or not you are?

My clients often wonder the same thing. They feel their CPAs are great at doing their taxes, but are the CPAs letting their clients know when they could make a change to help them save money?

I have found that many tax preparers are so busy at tax time that they don't do any tax planning. Most CPAs are great at getting the right numbers in the right boxes, but when it comes to proactive planning, most of my clients have felt they were underserved.

So my firm set out to fix that problem by creating Parker Tax Advisors and establishing a strategic relationship with a local team of CPAs. Our clients now have access to high-quality CPAs to prepare their tax returns.

After the CPA prepares the tax return, a second CPA will review the return for accuracy. After the tax return is complete, the CPAs send it to our firm for a review. While we rely on our CPAs to make sure they record history properly, we spend time reviewing our clients' returns for future tax planning. Once we review a client's return, we then schedule a time to have our client pick-up the tax return, review it, and schedule a tax planning session if needed.

I ask prospective clients, "When was the last time your CPA talked to your financial advisor?" and they say, "Never." When planning your financial life, shouldn't the left hand know what the right hand is doing? We think so. So we created Parker Tax Advisors to help fix this problem for the people we serve.

How you structure your investments for maximum tax efficiency is also important. It doesn't make sense to hold a tax-deferred fixed annuity in an IRA for tax purposes. However Fixed Indexed Annuities/Hybrids might be a good fit in an IRA.

Of course, a double tax deferral account doesn't exist, but we are not using the Fixed Indexed Annuity for tax deferral. It is an instrument to allow for growth without risking the principal based on market fluctuations. It often makes sense to hold your safe and hybrid investments in your IRA and hold your growth/equity positions in your taxable accounts.

Why? Well, if you are going to lose money, would you rather lose money in your IRA account or your non-qualified account?

You could capture those losses in the non-qualified account on your tax return. Or if the growth account is primarily held in equity positions, then the IRS, in most instances, would tax the growth with long-term capital gains rates, which are currently lower than ordinary income tax rates, saving you money.

If you have bonds or income producing assets as a part of your portfolio or decide to add bonds to your portfolio, then you should consider holding them inside your IRA or Roth IRA because they are then tax-deferred or tax free so you won't be getting a pesky 1099 at the end of every year, but only when you actually pull out the money from the IRA.

Remember that tax preparation is different than tax planning. Keep in mind it's not how much you make—it's how much you keep. Be sure to find an advisor who understands and studies the income tax system and incorporates tax planning into his or her advice.

Chapter 6

CAN I AFFORD TO RETIRE?

My prospective clients often ask, "Can I afford to retire?" I have found that retirement is all about cash flow, not net worth. Especially after the real estate crash, I have met people who may have a net worth of $2 million, which looks great on paper, but when it comes to retirement income, they are just barely squeaking by on their social security and a small pension. It's great that you are worth $2 million, but ultimately, it's your cash flow that will determine your quality of life in retirement, not your net worth.

In order to do justice to a retirement plan and confidently answer the question, "Do I have enough?" it is critical that you understand your expenses. Most people don't want to and are not going to carry around an iPhone and enter and categorize every transaction in their lives—like I mentioned that I do. So I have found a free Internet tool that can do the categorizing for you at **www.mint.com**.

Mint will automatically grab transactions from your bank account and categorize them for you. To get the full effect, try to use your debit card and no cash for ninety days on purchases so you can really dial into this tool. After ninety days, **www.mint.com** will have very detailed reports to help break down how much money you are spending every month and where that money is going.

It's always a shocker to see just how much of my money my local grocery store, Central Market in Poulsbo, is getting. Now I know some of you are thinking "This is just a little too Big Brotherish for me." And I have to admit that even for a geeky techno financial advisor, I was a bit hesitant to trust providing so much of my personal information over the Internet. But I got over it, and so far so good. I have been very pleased with how this budgeting tool works. If this method seems a little too high tech for some of you, another alternative is to do it the old school way. The old school way may not be as accurate, but it will get you going in the right direction. For those of you who are looking for a good old fashioned paper budget data gathering form, I have included one on our website at **www.thriving-in-retirement.com**.

Retirement is all about cash flow not net worth. The most successful retirees I know have learned to live within their means. It's critical that we establish your budget so we can accurately determine how much retirement income you are going to need. The first goal of a good retirement income plan will be to guarantee anywhere from 70 to 100 percent of the income needed to maintain your basic living needs on an inflation adjusted basis.

VOLATILITY AND YOUR TIME HORIZON

You have probably heard the saying, "Don't worry; the market goes up and down, but over a long period of time it goes up." That is a true statement, but it's important to understand your time horizon versus the market's time horizon.

Retirees start to question this age-old wisdom when the market takes a turn for the worse like it did in 2008 because they realize they may not have fifteen, twenty, or even thirty years for the market to recoup. If you are relying on your investment portfolio to generate an income stream to supplement your other retirement income, it becomes increasingly important to be protected against such volatility.

I recently ran an online calculator for a male, age seventy, to determine life expectancy. His life expectancy was eighty-three, which establishes a basic time horizon to work with. Now we can start building a retirement strategy around some reasonable assumptions. If these numbers are correct, should he have 100 percent of his assets in growth stocks if the purpose of the money is to generate consistent and reliable income? No.

On the following page is a chart of the Dow Jones Industrial Average (DJIA) from the early 1900s to the present. As you can see from the lines I have drawn, historically long periods exist when the DJIA index traded sideways, showing no gain and no loss. The most significant years were from 1929 to 1954. The market crashed in 1929, beginning the Great Depression. Notice that it took the market twenty-five years to recoup. Imagine if you had retired in 1929 and had all of your money invested in stocks. YIKES. Then you heard your broker say, "Don't worry Mr. and Mrs. Jones, the market goes up; it always does over a long period of time." Your time horizon isn't getting longer as you get older. It is getting shorter, so it makes sense to reduce your exposure to the market's volatility as time marches on.

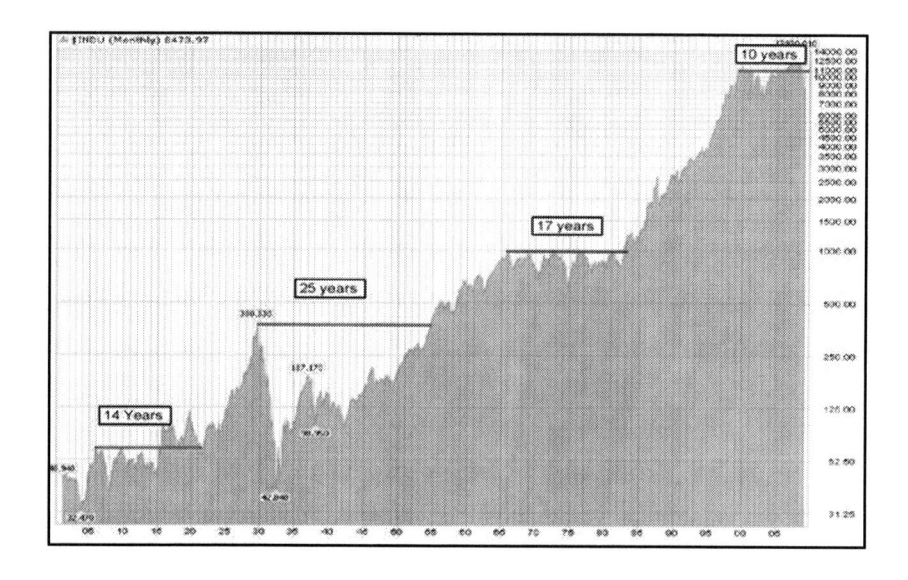

Not long ago, a prospective client of mine came in for a second opinion on her investment portfolio. Her assets had nose-dived during 2008, and she had asked her broker to put her into a "safer" position. He moved her into bonds, which I've already told you are not "safe" by my definition, but that wasn't the worst of it. She was eighty years old and could probably expect to live to be ninety. Since her broker had sold her twenty-year bonds, if she would need that money during her lifetime, she would have to cash in the bonds early and possibly pay a penalty on them. If she died without needing the money, her beneficiaries would have to wait the additional ten years before they could liquidate the bonds without a loss. When I told this story to Jane Bryant Quinn, one of the nation's leading commentators on personal finance whom I interviewed on my radio show, her only comment was, "That man should be in jail."

You need to understand your own life expectancy. If you are in great health, exercise regularly, and have a family history of longevity, then you should plan to live a longer life. One of my favorite online tools for determining life expectancy is **www.livingto100.com**.

INVESTMENT WORLDS

Imagine you are seventy years old with a comfortable retirement and a $1 million nest egg. You are drawing $40,000 per year to supplement your retirement pension and social security income. Everything is going great, and your financial advisor says all is well since your withdrawal rate is at only about 4 percent; according to most financial professionals, that is a safe level of withdrawal at which you would not risk depleting your life savings.

You have followed your financial advisor's recommendation and diversified your investments among stocks, bonds, mutual funds, and ETFs. Then 2008 hits and suddenly you face one of the worst recessions since the Great Depression. In one year, you watch your life savings drop from $1 million to less than $500,000. Your financial advisor calls you into his office and explains that you are now draining your portfolio at 8 percent per year, and at the rate you are going, a much higher possibility exists that you will run out of money before you reach the end of your life.

You then have to choose between two frightening options: Would you like to cut your retirement income in half? Or risk running out of money? Frankly, I don't like either of these options and neither should you.

Understanding the different investment worlds you can use to diversify your investment assets is important in building your investment strategy for retirement. Many advisors hunker down under one investment philosophy, and they refuse to look at the alternatives that exist. However, in these situations, financial advisors need to get their egos out of the way.

The plan I put together for a client isn't about me. It's about my client achieving his or her goals, dreams, and aspirations, and doing so with the highest degree of confidence in an investment plan. To give my client that confidence, I have to be flexible in my thinking and evaluate opportunities as they show up.

The investment and financial planning world is geared toward stocks, bonds, and mutual funds. The recommendation of these particular vehicles seems to stems from an inherent conflict of interest that exists in our profession. Most financial advisors have underlying self-interests in the recommendations they are making. Sometimes as a client, you don't know whether the advice you are getting is really in your best interest or in your advisor's best interest.

In my firm, I recommend my clients diversify across three different investment worlds: Safety, Growth, and Hybrids.

THE WORLD OF SAFETY

Three institutions make up this world of safety: banks, governments, and insurance companies. If you go to a bank and say, "Mr. Banker, I want my money safe, guaranteed, and earning the highest rate of return," the banker will recommend CDs. The government will offer U.S. Savings bonds, and insurance companies will offer deferred fixed annuities. All three investment vehicles share common characteristics. First, your principal is protected from loss. Second, you earn a fixed rate of interest. And finally, if you want to draw your money out of these accounts before the end of the term, you will pay a penalty/surrender charge for early withdrawal. These options are ultra conservative and very boring. They also provide a low rate of return on your money.

THE WORLD OF GROWTH

Three institutions participate in the growth world: mutual fund companies, brokerage firms, and insurance companies. If you go to a mutual fund company and say, "Mr. Mutual Fund, I want my money to outpace inflation," a mutual fund company is going to recommend a mutual fund from its company. If you call up Vanguard for example, its advisors will likely recommend a Vanguard index mutual fund.

Brokerage firms will offer a variety of investment tools that are large and growing: stocks, bonds, mutual funds, ETF's, REITS, limited partnerships, commodities, hedge funds, and the list goes on. Insurance companies will offer variable annuities.

Insurance companies work in both the growth and safe worlds. On the safe side of the equation, they offer fixed annuities and on the growth side variable annuities. A variable annuity is a bunch of mutual funds wrapped inside an annuity contract.

Growth world investments share a couple of characteristics. First, your principal is not guaranteed. Second, you will earn a variable rate of return, and finally, if you really want to take advantage of the world of growth, you need TIME on your side.

When you are investing in the world of potential/growth, you need to understand the historical volatility of the stock market. Look at a chart of the S&P 500 on a daily basis. You see very sharp peaks and valleys. Wild swings in market volatility, on a short-term basis, are expected. If you stand back and look at a chart of the S&P 500 during a fifteen-year time horizon, you will notice the volatility is much less extreme. You'll see a gradual climb up instead of the peaks and valleys. Ultimately, TIME is the cure to volatility in the stock market. The more time you have on your side, the more volatility your investment portfolio can handle. Remember, too, stocks have never lost money during a fifteen-year period, as measured by the S&P 500.

Earlier in this book, I discussed your time horizon versus the market's time horizon. If you are seventy-five years old and your life expectancy is eighty-four, you may not have enough time to participate in the world of growth.

The term growth is used interchangeably with the words equity and risk throughout this book.

THE WORLD OF HYBRIDS

In the mid-1990s, insurance companies began to develop products to fit the space between CDs and mutual funds. Banks and brokerage companies quickly hopped on board the bandwagon by creating their own hybrid products.

Insurance companies developed the hybrid by taking the three elements of fixed annuities: safety of principal, a guaranteed fixed rate of return, and surrender/penalty charges for early withdrawal, and linking them to an external indices/stock index such as the S&P 500, creating the Fixed Index Annuity. This type of annuity can be designed for growth but not necessarily an income stream. Fixed Index Annuities (FIA) are also referred to as ratchet annuities because, like a ratchet, they can only go one way—up! So you can never lose your principal. However, hybrids usually cap your gain by setting a limit to the amount you can earn. For example, if you had invested money in an FIA with an 8 percent cap and the stock market soared to 14 percent during that year, you'd be limited to 8 percent of the 14 percent growth. This scenario assumes you are using an annual point-to-point strategy with a cap. Many different crediting strategies are available within these contracts, but this one is the easiest to understand, and the one I most frequently recommend.

You're probably thinking, "Well, that's crummy. I want to earn the 14 percent." But remember, you also can't lose anything on a down year. So if the stock market goes down the next year, you stay at 0 percent growth and 0 percent loss.

Let's assume you have an FIA with an 8 percent cap linked to the S&P 500, and during the course of one year, the S&P 500 increased by 10 percent; then your index annuity would credit you with an 8 percent interest rate for the year. The great thing about that 8 percent return is that it is now locked in, and you can't lose that gain based on future stock market performance. So if you had $100,000 dollars invested in one of these hybrids, and you earned 8 percent based on the performance of the market at the end of the first contract year, you would have $108,000.

But the real power of the index annuity is displayed in years when the stock market declines. For example, let's say in the second year of the contract, the S&P 500 fell by 10 percent. Remember, your annuity has grown to $108,000. In a year when the market declines by 10 percent, you don't lose a penny. You don't make anything in that year, but you don't lose either. The hybrids are a good tool to help you fight inflation. Insurance companies offer Fixed Indexed Annuities. Banks offer equity linked CDs and brokerage companies offer indexed notes.

All these vehicles are similar because they are designed to protect your principal while giving you the opportunity to earn a rate of return greater than you might earn in a traditional fixed rate account. Of the three available, I believe the annuity version is best-suited for most retirees primarily because of the liquidity features and guaranteed returns available on the annuity versus the other instruments that are available.

In a recent study by Jack Marrion, Geoffrey VanderPal, and David Babbel from Wharton School of business[1], he argued that these hybrids/FIAs have performed favorably during the past ten years. Granted, the last ten years the stock market has had a bad run.

---

[1] Marrion, Jack et al. Wharton Financial Institutions Center Personal Finance: Real World Index Annuity Returns. October, 5 2009. http://www.nafa.com/resources/nafa-file-archives/2009/doc_download/613-2009-wfic-real-world-index-annuity-returns.html Accessed February 25, 2011

But that's precisely why these tools were created. Because we can't begin to guess what the stock market will do, the hybrid is a way to have some upside exposure to the market while protecting your principal.

Hybrids are an alternative to traditional fixed income/safe vehicles such as CDs or bonds, but they should not be a replacement for your equity/growth positions. As of this writing, the U.S. Federal Government has set the federal funds rate at essentially 0 percent. When interest rates begin to climb, bond holders could see a significant loss if they have to liquidate their bonds before maturity. But with an FIA, you always know the worst case position if you have to exit your contract early, whereas, with bonds you have more unknowns and more volatility. If the anticipated return for the fixed income portion of your portfolio is only somewhere between 4 and 6 percent, and if both a bond portfolio and a Fixed Indexed Annuity have performed within that range, shouldn't you choose to use the safer of the two tools?

HOW MUCH RISK SHOULD YOU TAKE?

Let's take a look at how you can use the tools within each of these different worlds to create a plan to provide you with a good balance of safety and growth so you can protect your assets from stock market risk and still help protect your assets from inflation risk.

Many advisors use the Age-100 rule of thumb to determine how much of your investment portfolio should be invested in risk positions versus how much should be invested in safe positions. It's a simple equation and may not be an appropriate mix depending on the purpose of your money. You may need to be more or less aggressive to ensure you don't run out of money. But let's use the rule of Age-100 as a starting point.

Take your current age and subtract it from 100. Let's say you are sixty, so if you subtract that from 100, it equals forty. According to the Age-100 rule, you would want 40 percent of your liquid assets invested in growth/risk position (a position that battles inflation but where you can also lose money), and 60 percent in a safety position (a position that protects your principal).

The closer you get to age 100, the more money you want in safe positions since you are transitioning through retirement and are running out of time. Remember, time is the ultimate cure for the volatility of your growth/risk accounts. As you get older, it becomes more important to protect against market risk than it does to protect against inflation risk.

While stock market volatility can erode your principal overnight, inflation is usually a slow moving train that eats away at your buying power over time. Both risks are real and important, but I want to make sure you diversify appropriately given your time horizon rather than the market's time horizon.

Run this calculation for yourself. Then take a look at your investments to see whether they match up with this rule for diversifying. Many people will find the majority of their money is still in a growth position. I see many people with 70 to 90 percent of their retirement assets invested in growth vehicles. Many portfolios generally have a mix of stocks, bonds, mutual funds, and a little cash, and those folks assume they have a properly diversified portfolio. They don't, and I believe not understanding what makes up a properly diversified portfolio is one of the biggest mistakes many investors make.

You will notice that stocks and bonds are vehicles that are both situated in the world of growth, which is fine when you are younger, have time on your side, or are in an upward trending market. But in a year like 2008, where treasuries were the only asset class not losing money, focusing solely on growth is a crummy strategy. It's not uncommon for me to hear stories about people who lost 30 percent or more of their retirement savings by having most of their money in growth positions.

DON'T PUT ALL YOUR EGGS IN ONE BASKET

Recently, I was watching a TV program where the host was discussing investing and taking telephone calls from viewers. A man called and said, "I have three stocks, they are blank, blank, and blank. Am I diversified? The host said, "Um, let's see. You have energy, entertainment, and medical," or something like that and then said, "Boy, that is GREAT. That is one of the best diversified portfolios I have seen."

That isn't a direct quote, but the situation was close enough to that. Now if I were investing my clients' retirement life savings using this model of diversification, I wouldn't sleep very well at night. Unfortunately, when I meet with many people for the first time, they tell me, "Oh yes, I'm diversified. My advisor told me I am." Then I start to dig around a little and find they aren't diversified at all.

When I was a boy, my dad used to say that diversification means not putting all of your eggs in one basket. I have carried that advice with me, and I now use an award-winning system to help ensure my clients don't have all of their eggs in one basket or in this case investment worlds.

Some clients believe they are diversified because they are following the age-100 rule so at age sixty they have $100,000 with $60,000 in bonds and $40,000 in an equity mutual fund. Can you lose money in bonds? If you had money invested in bonds in 2008, you know you can. We even saw some people lose money in the money market accounts in the great crash of 2008. So if you can lose money in bonds would that qualify as a safe place? NO. NO. NO. **A growth position, in my definition, is any investment where you can lose money**. Some people only refer to stocks as growth, but I also refer to bonds as growth because you can lose money. Many people own mutual funds, but they don't know what each of those mutual funds is invested in. So according to the example above, they have all $100,000 in risk vehicles where they can lose money.

Fixed income vehicles do exist that have historically performed at about the same rate as a bond portfolio but your principal is protected from loss. Remember, you're retired now. You're not contributing anything more to the nest egg you have accumulated. What you have is what you have, and it may need to last a very long time in retirement. Be cautious if your advisor talks to you about diversification and you have a large percentage of your so called "SAFE MONEY" invested in bonds. It may be time for a second opinion.

DIVERSIFYING YOUR TIME HORIZON AND INVESTMENT SELECTION

Don't bring a knife to a gun fight.
— Author Unknown

I frequently find people who have a brokerage account with a mix of stocks and bonds and are following the Age-100 rule. We've already discussed why I don't believe bonds are safe, so let's assume these people, at my advice, have moved their accounts from bonds to truly "safe" tools, but I don't believe they should stop there. I believe they should take their diversification strategy one step further.

Instead of just diversifying across growth and safe accounts, you should also diversify your time horizon. This strategy is especially important for retirees who need their savings to supplement their incomes. By diversifying your time horizon, you are allocating your assets across multiple segments with each segment having a specific goal. If you were building a deck and wanted to screw the decking down, you wouldn't use a hammer to do the job. The same is true with each segment of your investment strategy. What you want to do is to use the best tool for the job at hand.

Let's say you are sixty years old and you plan on living to age ninety. You should diversify your investments across six time segments. Each segment would have a specific goal. The key to this diversification strategy is to understand that time is the only real cure to the stock market's volatility. Essentially, this diversification strategy is designed to buy time.

The first segment will be your least risky and might have a five-year time horizon associated with it. This segment is the money you plan to use for immediate income needs so you cannot take any risk at all with these assets. You are looking at laddering CDs, using money market accounts, or single premium immediate annuities. Your ultimate goal for the first segment is safety of principal, and your second objective is return.

Your next segment is constructed for years five to ten. Because you have a little more time on your side, you can afford to take a little more risk. But you still want a high degree of safety for this second stage because you know that at the end of the first five years, you are going to need to rely on these investments to continue to provide for income. But again, you are buying time. Because you know you won't need this money for five years, you can afford to take more risks. You are less concerned with liquidity. You can ladder five-year CDs, or consider fixed annuities, or if you are willing to take a little more risk, you can buy highly rated individual corporate bonds or government bonds with a five-year maturity. You would continue to construct an investment strategy using multiple segments with each segment using the best tool for its specific purpose.

By the time you are at the sixth segment, you know you will have a thirty-year time horizon. With this money, you can afford to take the most risk because you know you won't have to touch these assets for thirty years.

A TRULY AGE-BASED DIVERSIFIED PORTFOLIO

How do you implement your investment strategy? Let's assume you are seventy years old, and you have decided you want to keep 70 percent of your money in safe positions and 30 percent of your money in a growth position. By doing so, you have created a strategy to help protect you from the two primary risks to your money: market risk and inflation.

But how would you use the hybrid world? I'd recommend that you put 35 percent in the safety world, 35 percent in the hybrid world, and 30 percent in the growth world.

Let's assume a CD earning 3 percent is in the safe account. In the hybrid account, let's use a Fixed Indexed Annuity that has an 8 percent point-to-point annual cap. In the growth account, we will use an investment portfolio with 60 percent geared toward tactical asset allocation and 40 percent geared toward strategic asset allocation. Let's see how this diversification strategy would have held up in 2008, one of the worst years in the stock market's history.

As we begin to explore performance, please keep in mind that past performance is no guarantee of future results. I'd like to focus more on the process rather than the performance.

Your safe CD earned 3 percent. Your hybrid Fixed Indexed Annuity earned 0 percent, and your growth account invested in the stock market lost 7.11 percent. If you had started in January 2008 with $100,000, at the end of the year, your $100,000 would be worth $98,917. Nobody likes to lose money. But remember this was one of the worst years in the market's history. It's not uncommon for me to hear about retirees who lost up to 50 percent of their investments. So after one of the worst years in the market, your $100,000 initial investment has lost only -1.08 percent. Most of my clients understand that no matter how well they diversify, some years they will lose their money, and they still sleep at night when they are only down a little more than 5 percent in a year.

But let's also look at a good year in the market and see how your investment portfolio would have performed. Again assuming you started with $100,000 on January 1, 2009, your CD is only earning 3 percent. Your hybrid account can go up with the market but not down, so in a good year like 2009, you earned an 8 percent return, and your investment portfolio was up 19.88 percent. So at the end of 2009, your investment account is now worth $109,814 up from $100,000. That is a 9.8 percent return.

In a year like 2008, when many people lost 40 percent or more of their investments, would you be content with a -1.08 percent loss? And in a good year, would you be happy with a 9.8 percent gain? Are you accomplishing your goal of protecting assets from the down side of the market while giving your portfolio enough opportunity for growth to keep pace with inflation?

DIVERSIFYING WITHIN YOUR GROWTH WORLD: THE ART AND SCIENCE OF INVESTING

We've talked about diversifying or laddering your investments across the three different worlds of: safety, growth, and hybrid, and across your time horizon, but you also want to diversify within your growth accounts. For my clients' equity positions, I use two systems for diversifying their growth assets, one of which won the Nobel Prize in economics. When I tell my clients their equity positions are diversified, I have a proven system I use for monitoring and comparing their portfolios. I constantly monitor the asset allocation and the money managers and make adjustments any time my clients' portfolios fall outside of their desired asset allocation. This style of institutional money management is newly available to the average investor. One of the reasons I started Parker Financial is because I believe every investor should have access to the same tools and resources the ultra rich have.

I subscribe to two different philosophies that can be combined for how you can invest your money in the stock market:

- Tactical Investment Management — The Art of Investing
- Strategic Asset Allocation — The Science of Investing

We'll take a look at each of these below. I recognize that some people will believe strongly about one or the other investment style so much so that they will be unwilling to bend or see investing from the other perspective. For some, it's all or nothing. But I believe both of these styles are justifiable for different reasons. I tell my clients both are good investment styles, and depending on market conditions, different strategies will perform better than others.

When it comes to my clients' retirement savings and investment plans working, I'd rather be right 50 percent of the time than wrong 100 percent of the time. With the current extreme volatility we are seeing in the market, I am recommending that clients take a more active approach to managing their investments.

Depending on a client's risk tolerance, goals and objectives, I recommend having 60 percent allocated toward a tactical (art) hands-on approach and 40 percent allocated to a strategic (scientific) indexing approach.

TACTICAL INVESTMENT MANAGEMENT

In tactical investment management, the managers are seeking opportunities to avoid risk by actively trading and managing a portfolio, which means they will, at times, move your investments out of the stock market. This style of management is the "art" side of investing. It can't be academically or scientifically proven, but some managers have had very impressive results over a long period of time. Even though no guarantees exist that these results will continue into the future, you would be hard-pressed to discount what some of the tactical money managers have achieved. As of September 30, 2010, one of our tactical money manager's ten-year returns was 10.08 percent. Not too shabby. But what's even more impressive is that in the past ten years, this particular money manager has not had a year on an annualized basis, where money was lost. Now there were some years where this money manager greatly under-performed the index, but many of my clients aren't concerned with beating an index. What they tell me they want is to keep their money working for them to protect them as much as possible against the downside risk of the stock market while giving them the best opportunity to beat inflation. My firm likes to work with tactical money management teams that have a proven record for demonstrating their ability to do just that.

STRATEGIC ASSET ALLOCATION

Strategic asset allocation was born through Modern Portfolio Theory (MPT). Harry Markowitz and William F. Sharpe won the Nobel Prize in 1990 for developing this theory. Modern Portfolio Theory proposes how rational investors will use diversification to optimize their portfolios, and how a risk asset should be priced. Modern Portfolio Theory assumes that investors are risk adverse, meaning that given two assets that offer the same expected return, investors will prefer the less risky one. Thus, an investor will take on increased risk only if compensated by higher expected returns. Conversely, an investor who wants higher returns must accept more risk. The exact trade-off will differ by investor, based upon individual risk aversion characteristics. The implication is that a rational investor will not invest in a portfolio if a second portfolio exists with a more favorable risk-return profile—i.e., if for that level of risk an alternative portfolio exists, which has better expected returns, the rational investor will choose it. A landmark study conducted in 1991 and expanded in 1993 suggests that portfolio asset allocation is the most important long-term determinant of investment results. Strategic asset allocation also suggests that no one can accurately and consistently predict when shifts in market leadership will occur or how long they will last. The market leaders of one year often become the laggards the next. Strategic asset allocation, therefore, suggests that it's important to spread your assets across multiple investment asset classes so you can potentially benefit from an upswing in any one asset class. It also suggests that the stock market is efficient and that all asset classes do not move in tandem. So the hope is that when one asset class zigs, the other zags, because we are looking for balance between these asset classes. In 2008 when the market went haywire, this type of strategy didn't work very well. The only negatively correlated asset class was treasuries. Typically, when stocks drop, bonds increase. But because of the fear in 2008, even high quality bond mutual funds lost money. Many of those bond funds made a strong recovery once people got their senses back and fear resided.

CONCLUSION: REBALANCING YOUR PORTFOLIO

Buy low; sell high. That's easy to do if you systematically rebalance your portfolio. What really makes strategic asset allocation work properly is a systematic approach to rebalancing. Rebalancing forces you to sell high and buy low. Because you are broadly diversified among asset classes, some years some asset classes will do better than others. Many different thoughts exist about how and when to rebalance a portfolio, but as a general rule, we tend to rebalance when an asset class is more than a certain percent out of its threshold.

Rebalancing is a systematic way to ensure you are forced to sell some of your winners and buy more of your losers. It's the ultimate contrarian play because you believe markets are efficient, and eventually, a reversion will happen to the mean so that one asset class won't always be a leader or laggard, and you want to have exposure to it when it begins to move to doing well because different asset classes will perform better under different market conditions.

Many academic articles have been written on Modern Portfolio Theory and the benefits of strategic asset allocation. It is scientifically recognized, and many of the greatest minds in finance will argue that it is the only way to invest your money. It has a proven track record and is used by many large institutions for managing billions of dollars.

However, both of these investment styles offer advantages and disadvantages. Market conditions will determine which one of these two styles will perform the best. In an upward trending market like we had from the early 1980s to 1999, strategic asset allocation will probably perform best. In a very volatile market like we had in 2008, tactical asset allocation has performed better. They are both good, and as I said, I'd rather be right 50 percent of the time than wrong 100 percent of the time.

Chapter 7

THE IMPORTANCE OF FEES

Stop paying high commissions and fees for your mutual funds. Just stop it!

Okay, I've got that out of my system so let's move on. You need to understand the impact fees can have on your investment portfolio. I believe by diversifying your investments as suggested in the previous chapters, you are diversifying your investments for safety and growth, but you are also moving your investments to very fee-efficient accounts. If you had all your investments in no-load mutual funds, and the average fee on those mutual funds was 1 percent per year on $100,000, your annual expense would be $1,000. If you utilize my method for diversifying your investments, and we use the 35 percent safe, 35 percent hybrid, and 30 percent growth strategy, your annual ongoing fee would be $600 per year. Of course, that is assuming I am managing the growth investments for you and charging a 2 percent annual fee on those investments. Using simple math with no compounding, if you were saving $400 per year in fees, after ten years you would have an extra $4,000. If you currently own mutual funds, it can be hard to uncover all of the fees you are paying. Of course, your prospectus will list fees, but a quick way to help uncover all of the fees you are paying is to use a tool at **www.personalfund.com**.

EXCHANGE TRADED FUNDS (ETFS) VS. MUTUAL FUNDS

I am fan of low cost investing using asset allocation as the foundation for maximizing risk adjusted returns. Jack Bogle of Vanguard is one of my personal heroes in our industry and an advocate for the smaller investor. Vanguard built its firm around low cost Indexed Mutual Funds (IMFs), and now Vanguard is one of the leaders in the Exchange Traded Funds (ETFs) arena. Both vehicles have advantages and disadvantages.

One common complaint about ETFs is the brokerage fees associated with buying and selling these investments. If you intend to do a lot of buying and selling within the portfolio of ETFs, then you should use a more fee-efficient tool to track an index, like the ETFs' close cousin the Index Mutual Fund, instead.

However, I have found ETFs have lower costs, are more liquid, and can be very tax efficient, which is very important for your non-qualified accounts. Either choice serves the same basic purpose. Both are excellent vehicles for achieving your long-term growth goals.

ETFs and IMFs are both very efficient tools for creating global broad-based diversified portfolios among asset classes and sectors, and they should be considered as a part of your overall diversification strategy.

Chapter 8

DIVERSIFYING IN A RETIREMENT INCOME STRATEGY

I've explained the different investment worlds, and how to create a diversified portfolio. Let's use the same concepts but build a portfolio for retirement **income**. In an earlier example, I talked about a seventy year old client whose investments I split into three separate and unique sectors, each one with a specific return goal. Each segment also had a specific time horizon, and as his time horizon increased, so did the propensity to take on additional risk to earn a greater return.

By diversifying assets by time as well as risk, you create a high probability for success. At my firm, I want to know how my clients feel about risk. If I have an ultra-conservative client who is not comfortable at all with stock market risk, then I recommend a very conservative strategy. If a client has a higher propensity for risk, then I recommend a strategy that provides for the opportunity to earn the greatest return. Let's take a look at both approaches.

THE ULTRA CONSERVATIVE APPROACH TO GUARANTEED RETIREMENT INCOME

For clients who are ultra conservative, I find they sleep better at night if I use tools that help provide guarantees. For example,

John and Sally are both seventy-three, and they have a total of $500,000. They need the $500,000 to provide them with $20,000 dollars of income for the rest of their lives, and they are ULTRA conservative.

First, I could take $128,895 and purchase a Single Premium Immediate Annuity (SPIA) contract that is guaranteed to pay for a seven-year period. This contract provides the clients with a guaranteed annual income stream of $20,000. But the clients prefer to have the income monthly so they receive $1,666 per month for the next seven years. A single premium immediate annuity is sometimes called a pension annuity because it provides a monthly income for seven years. At the end of the seven years, the income stops and the $128,895 is gone.

The clients have spent all the money. Of the original $500,000 we had to work with, I also used $213,733 to fund the second segment of the plan, which is turned on after the first segment has completed paying out. In segment two, I use a Fixed Indexed Annuity (FIA or Hybrid) contract with a Lifetime Income Benefit Rider (LIBR). The LIBR has two important guarantees: First, it guarantees the clients' income account value will compound and grow at 8 percent per year until they start drawing income. Second, when they turn the income stream on, the insurance company guarantees a payout that is, in part, based on the clients' age.

So in this example, after seven years of income from the SPIA, the clients will now be eighty years old. Their FIA with the LIBR rider has grown to $384,615, and they now flip the switch to begin the income stream. This particular contract is based on the younger of the two people, but since they are both eighty, the contract guarantees they can now withdraw 6.5 percent per year of the Income Account Value (IAV) which is $384,615, meaning they will have $25,000 per year in income or $2,083 per month.

The clients are also now receiving a raise to account for inflation. If we assume an inflation of 3 percent per year for the last seven years, the clients now needs $25,000 per year to replace what had been $20,000 per year. The nice thing about using the LIBR is the clients are not forced to annuitize their contract. The clients remain in control. A major drawback to annuitization is when the annuitant dies, any funds remaining in the contract may go to the insurance company. You can find ways to work around this issue, but none are completely satisfactory.

The $25,000 of annual income is guaranteed for as long as both people are alive, even if the account value is depleted. I was able to guarantee the income the clients needed for the rest of their lives using only $342,628 out of the $500,000 they started with. Because they don't need the $157,372 for their retirement income, they can take a more aggressive approach with this money and invest it in the stock market.

Let's say the clients end up living to age 100. If they earned 7 percent per year on their $157,372, their growth account would have grown to approximately $1 million.

The emphasis of this type of planning is on guaranteeing income for life. Retirement is really all about cash flow and not net worth. Your income is what allows you to do the things you want to do. If you can solve for income first, then you are less concerned about the fluctuations and stock market volatility, and more likely to stick with your investment strategy through the bad times.

THE MORE AGGRESSIVE APPROACH TO RETIREMENT INCOME

Since the above system seems to work great, why would you need to have an alternative? Some people I work with have an aversion to certain tools or products. I have people who come into our office who are absolutely opposed to using annuities. Either they have had a bad experience with them, or they have read enough of the media garbage that they aren't willing to consider them in their plan. I'm fine with that. You need to let your advisor know about these concerns or aversions before a plan is built. If a client tells me he doesn't like or understand annuities and would prefer not to use them, then I have alternatives.

Let's take the same scenario as before but use fewer annuities to construct the plan. Even if you prefer not to use a Fixed Indexed Annuity with the LIBR, I still like the single Premium Immediate Annuity to provide you with income for the first segment of the plan. Insurance companies designed these tools to provide income. They don't require maintenance or meddling. They are simple, easy, and fee-efficient.

Maybe instead, you use a five-year SPIA instead of a seven-year in the first segment. Then in the second segment, you would use a tactical money management conservative portfolio. In the third segment, you would also use a tactical money manager with a conservative growth asset allocation. The fourth and fifth segments, because you have the most time on your side, would use a strategic asset allocation moderate growth strategy and strategically rebalance.

The key is to have a plan and make sure you are working with an advisor who understands the difference between how you should invest your money when accumulating assets versus establishing a plan for the distribution and income phase of your retirement life. Find someone who is flexible and has the ability to do things the way you want them done.

My clients should view me as a coach. They tell me what it is they are trying to accomplish, and I show them a couple of different ways they can achieve their goals. If I am the coach, ultimately, they are the general managers and have to decide which way is best for them.

Chapter 9

TIPS FOR MAXIMIZING YOUR SOCIAL SECURITY BENEFIT

When social security started, the average life expectancy was sixty-six. You couldn't start receiving your benefits until age sixty-five. So what started out as old-age insurance and wasn't expected to be paid to very many people has blossomed into a very important retirement benefit. For the baby boomer generation, it is more important than ever because the boomers don't generally have pensions. Now the boomers have to rely on social security and their savings for a lifetime of income.

Based on the 2010 statements you receive every year from the Social Security Administration, by 2016, social security won't be bringing in enough money to keep the system above water. By 2037, the year I am eligible for my social security benefits, social security will only be able to pay out 76 cents on the dollar. So by 2037, if you had been receiving $1,000 per month in benefits, it is possible social security would reduce your benefit to $760 per month.

If you have the forty credits of work required to qualify for your benefits, you can begin drawing your benefit at age sixty-two. However, by beginning at age sixty-two, your social security benefit will be about 25 percent less (for those born between 1943-1954) than it will be if you wait until your full retirement age, which for most baby boomers will be age sixty-six.

Every year you wait to start your benefits beyond age sixty-six increases your benefits by 8 percent. Remember, if you begin drawing benefits at age sixty-two, you are limited on how much income you can earn in one year before social security reduces your benefits. In 2009, you can earn $14,160. After the $14,160 threshold has been met, your benefits would be reduced by $1 for every $2 in other earnings. So if you plan to work beyond age sixty-two, it might make sense to delay taking your benefits.

Most boomers will be eligible for their full retirement benefits at age sixty-six. At this time, you can earn as much money as you like without worrying about your benefits being reduced. Nor are you required to take your benefits at age sixty-six. In fact, every month you wait to take them, you will earn bonus credits at about 0.66 percent more each month. If you were to delay taking your benefits until age seventy, you could have as much as 132 percent of your full retirement benefit.

Always file for your benefits at age sixty-six even if you want to delay taking the income. A little known portion of the social security rules allows you to "File and Suspend." This rule allows you to file for your benefits at age sixty-six, but suspend taking the payments. Perhaps you are planning to work until age seventy or beyond. I know I love my work, and I would hate to retire at age sixty-six. So by filing and suspending, you have some options you wouldn't otherwise have.

Your suspended social security benefits are continuing to earn delayed credits. So if at age sixty-nine, you find an incredible real estate opportunity, you can go to social security and ask for a lump sum of all the benefits you were eligible to receive from age sixty-six to sixty-eight. It's almost like having a little savings account growing for you in the event you need it, but you don't have to pay tax on the income until you actually receive it.

By using the "File and Suspend" method, your spouse, once he or she has reached full retirement age, can draw his or her spousal benefit, which is about 50 percent of your benefit based on the "File and Suspend" even though you are not receiving a social security benefit. Always file for your benefits at age sixty-six even if you don't plan on taking your social security until age seventy.

WHAT HAPPENS TO MY SOCIAL SECURITY WHEN I DIE?

If Mr. Smith is receiving $1,000 per month in social security income, and Mrs. Smith is receiving her spousal benefit of $500 dollars per month, then their total monthly benefit is $1,500 per month. If Mr. Smith dies, Mrs. Smith will stop receiving her benefit of $500 per month, and she will receive a step up to her husband's higher benefit (Survivor Benefit) making her total monthly income $1,000 per month. Because Mrs. Smith has a higher probability of living longer than Mr. Smith, they need to do some strategic planning to maximize the spousal benefit. If Mr. Smith delays taking his benefit until age seventy, they would maximize the amount of money available in retirement for Mrs. Smith.

Because boomers are likely going to rely more heavily on their social security benefits than past generations, they need to look at all of the different ways they can maximize these benefits and find a good advisor who can help them create a plan for taking those social security benefits.

Chapter 10

THE IRA LEGACY OPTIMIZER

I meet a lot of people today who tell me they live comfortably on their pension and their social security. Oftentimes, these folks have a sizeable amount of money in their IRA accounts, and that money's purpose is to pay for emergencies, occasional travel, putting a new roof on the house, or potentially buying a new car. These people have generally named their spouses as their beneficiaries and their children as their contingent beneficiaries, and most have never pulled money out of these accounts. So even though people are planning to use these tax deferred savings accounts as emergency funds, the reality is that they aren't being used at all. Why should that matter?

The IRS says that at age seventy-and-a-half, you are required to begin taking distributions from your IRA. This does not apply to a Roth IRA. When people take this distribution, if they don't need the money for living expenses, they will reinvest it in either a taxable investment account or certificates of deposit at the bank. Either way, they are creating an additional tax liability.

When you take your Required Minimum Distribution, you are taxed at your ordinary income tax rate, which is generally your highest rate as well. You then take the after-tax dollars and deposit them into your CDs at the bank. At the end of the year, you will receive a 1099 for the interest income earned on your CD. Even if you don't use the money and just reinvest it, you have to pay tax on the interest income.

Some people don't like the idea of using either savings bonds or tax-deferred fixed rate annuities to defer the interest income into the future because they believe taxes will likely go up, and they would rather pay tax rates at today's all-time low marginal rates, which makes sense. But an often overlooked opportunity exists. The money from your RMD can fund a life insurance policy.

If we assume you've had no withdrawals, and therefore, paid no taxes on your IRA, and we assume you are currently sixty years old and have a life expectancy of ninety, and your IRA is growing at 8 percent per year, then we can use the Rule of 72 to determine quickly that your IRA money will double every nine years. (A simple math trick is to divide 72 by your estimated average interest rate. For example 72/8=9.) So if you have $500,000, assuming no tax and no withdrawals and an 8 percent interest rate, your IRA balance at death would have doubled four times. Half a million dollars would double to $1 million by age sixty-nine. One million would double to $2 million by age seventy-eight. Two million would double to $4 million by age eighty-seven, and at age ninety, your $500,000 IRA would now be worth more than $5 million.

Do any of those numbers seem unrealistic? Is ninety a fair life expectancy for a healthy sixty year old today? Is it wild and crazy to think you could earn 8 percent on your money as an average during the next thirty years? No. All of these scenarios are highly probable today.

That is why Albert Einstein said, "The most powerful force in the universe is compound interest." Remember, your IRA is probably your most tax-hostile money. Every dollar you pull out of your IRA is going to be taxed at your ordinary income tax bracket (normally the highest). People say, "Yeah, but when I am retired, I'll be in a lower tax bracket." Do you really believe that?

In 2001, the Economic Growth and Tax Relief Act was passed, which lowered marginal income tax rates to historically low levels. The U.S. Government is spending money like crazy. Ten thousand baby boomers are retiring every single day and putting pressure on programs like Medicare and social security, which are already strained. And you, in your heart of hearts, believe taxes are going to stay at these all time low levels?

Let's assume they do. In the scenario above, you'd be leaving your children a $5 million IRA, which is potentially going to be subject to both estate tax and ordinary income tax. How would you feel about this?

Today, you have an IRA that is worth $500,000, and when you die thirty years from now, it may have grown to $5 million, and now Uncle Sam might collect 30 to 50 percent of that IRA money. How do you feel about leaving that much of your money to the government? Can you think of anything you would rather do with that money than give it to Uncle Sam? These are all just hypothetical numbers based on simple math and don't really work in the real world because the real world is much more complex. The IRS has rules about mandatory required minimum distributions, and our tax code changes every couple of years depending on who is elected, but this exercise gives you some big picture concepts or ideas to get you thinking. Once you have identified a problem, you need to look at some of the ways you might fix it.

Most people don't understand the benefits of life insurance. One of the reasons I like using life insurance for my clients is because it has the ability to pass income tax-free to your beneficiaries and potentially your estate, if done correctly. It is an incredibly efficient tool for transferring wealth out of your tax hostile IRA. A number of ways exist to structure these policies, but let me give you one quick example.

Let's say Mr. and Mrs. Miller are currently sixty-five years old, and Mr. Miller has $500,000 in his IRA. Mr. and Mrs. Miller don't need the IRA. It's just an emergency fund for travel and home repairs, and when they are both gone, the IRA will transfer to their son. Let's assume a very conservative 4 percent annual return on the money. When Mr. Miller turns seventy-and-a-half, he takes his required minimum distribution and pays the 35 percent tax. He then deposits the after tax amount into an account earning 4 percent. In twenty years, Mr. Miller's IRA and the taxable account into which he's been depositing his after tax RMD would have grown to $919,376. Assuming a 35 percent income tax at the time of death, Mr. Miller's son would receive $737,360 with $182,000 being lost to taxes.

Instead, let's say Mr. Miller begins taking 5 percent of his IRA beginning at age sixty-five, which out of $500,000 would be

$25,000 before taxes and approximately $18,750 after taxes at the 25 percent tax bracket.

Mr. Miller takes his after-tax IRA distribution of $18,750 to fund a guaranteed Second-to-Die Universal Life policy. In this case, he uses a second-to-die policy because it's the least expensive way to buy insurance, and it provides benefits to the heirs only after both spouses have died, which is what the Millers want since the primary purpose of the money is to leave it to their son. The $18,750 buys an income tax free death benefit of $1,450,593 using that life insurance policy.

If Mr. and Mrs. Miller were both to die in twenty years, then their after-tax gift to their son, under the first scenario, would be $737,360. By utilizing the life insurance in the second scenario and starting the distribution a few years earlier, the after-tax distribution would be $1,659,458 to their son. Their son would be inheriting 125 percent more after-taxes.

Life insurance has evolved over the years, and the new policies can come with some rather attractive features. For example, let's say you are seventy with a $500,000 IRA, and you have to begin taking your RMD. If you were to take the RMD, pay the tax due on it, and then roll the after-tax amount into a guaranteed life insurance contract, you would immediately have a death benefit of about $300,000. The life insurance policy would have a rider guaranteeing the death benefit would be good until age 120 as long as you made the minimum premium every year.

Both the cost of insurance and the death benefit is guaranteed so you don't have to worry about any surprises. Life insurance passes income tax free to your beneficiaries so, by using life insurance, you get out of the annual tax trap you have while holding CDs, dividend paying stocks, or mutual funds.

Some of these new life insurance policies also have long-term care and terminal illness riders giving you access of up to 80 percent of the death benefit in the event that you need long-term care or contract a terminal illness. These would also be tax free distributions.

The kicker with this type of planning is you have to be healthy enough to qualify for the policy. When it comes to life insurance planning, you should get these policies established as early and as young as possible so you don't have to worry about qualifying. I meet with people in their mid-seventies to early eighties, and they now want to use life insurance, but they can't qualify for coverage so it is no longer an option.

If you don't like life insurance, that's fine. Either way, the government is going to require you to pull money out of your IRA whether you want to or need to. The only question is what will you do with the after-tax money? You can roll that money into your CD or mutual fund, which will create an ongoing tax problem for you every year, or you can use the leverage of the life insurance to maximize the after-tax distribution to your heirs.

Chapter 11

LONG-TERM CARE INSURANCE— DO YOU REALLY NEED IT?

*I never want to be a burden to my children
either physically or financially.*

I hear this kind of statement over and over again, but when I bring up the topic of long-term care insurance, most people don't think they will ever need it. Those who do think they'll need it want to sit down with a planner and talk about the best way to plan for this potential event. Unfortunately, what they usually do is sit down with an insurance salesperson whose only goal is to sell a policy regardless of whether it is the right one for the individual person's situation.

So how do you plan for long-term care and should you consider long-term care insurance?

WHAT'S YOUR RISK?

A study by the U.S. Department of Health and Human Services says people who reach age sixty-five will have a 40 percent chance of entering a nursing home. About 10 percent of the people who enter a nursing home will stay there five years or more. Even with these staggering statistics, most people don't believe this situation will ever happen to them.

They'll argue their parents never needed care, they eat well and exercise regularly, and they are absolutely opposed to the idea they could ever lose their independence. Frankly, who can blame them? If you woke up every morning thinking your future existence might be one of dependence and ill health, why would you want to get out of bed?

To get an idea of what your risk might actually be, visit **www.medicare.gov** and use its long-term care calculator. You will be asked a series of questions regarding your health and family history; the calculator will then take all of this information and compare it to more than 40,000 people. It is looking for averages and similarities to try and understand your specific risk.

After analyzing the data, it will tell you what percentage of people with similar histories needed care and what percentage did not. It will also tell you the average time people similar to you spent in a nursing home and the average amount of money spent on that care. Once you have an idea of what your specific risks are, you can start to customize a plan of action.

WHAT ARE THE COSTS OF CARE?

Below are the national medians for home care, assisted living, and nursing homes taken from the Genworth 2010 cost of care survey.[1]

---

1 http://www.genworth.com/content/products/long_term_care/long_term_care/cost_of_care.html Accessed February 13, 2011.

- Home Care = $19 per hour = assuming full time 24 hours per day care = $166,440 per year

- Assisted Living = $3,185 per month = $38,220 per year

- Nursing Home = $206 dollars per day = $75,190 per year

Keep in mind that these numbers are as of April, 2010. Most of the people who are looking into this type of planning may not need care for fifteen to twenty-five more years. So if the cost today is $197,000 per year, then the cost of care in fifteen years will probably be closer to $400,000. You would have to come up with an additional $12,500 in monthly income for 2.8 years to cover this amount.

LONG-TERM CARE INSURANCE

Long-term Care (LTC) Insurance is expensive (although less so if you purchase it while you are still young), and you should own it. Early in my career, I was afraid to tell people they really needed to buy long-term care insurance. I didn't want to come across sounding like a pushy insurance salesperson. But life changes your opinions. I am now a very passionate advocate for long-term care insurance.

A good friend of mine, who was sixty years old at the time, was driving in his car when his driving became rather erratic. Some people called 911 to report a possible drunk driver. When the highway patrol arrived, they found my friend pulled off to the side of the road. He'd had a massive stroke. He has been on the road to recovery for a little more than a year and is now doing fairly well. However, he has lost most of his ability to move the right side of his body, and he has not regained his ability to speak yet.

This friend had been in great health. He had been a vegetarian for more than thirty years. He worked out and meditated three days per week. He was the last person I would have ever thought would need long-term care, and because of his health, I never suggested or recommended he consider long-term care insurance. But if I had, it would have greatly helped with covering the cost of his care.

A few years ago, a couple came to see me whom I asked whether they had long-term care insurance. They did not. I lightly suggested they consider looking into it. Two years went by, but they never followed up on getting any. Today, the wife has dementia, and they are paying a lot of money out of their retirement savings to help provide in-home care for her.

Unfortunately, when you specialize in working with retirees, you come across long-term care issues often. Because of these experiences, I have become a firm believer in long-term care insurance.

Some people are under the impression that they don't need to buy insurance. Their reasons are:

- The government will take care of me.
- My parents never needed long-term care.
- If I need care, my kids can take care of me.
- I exercise and eat right so I will never need long-term care.
- Long-term care insurance is too expensive.

- I will never go to a nursing home. I want to stay in my own home.

- I have enough money so I will self-insure against this risk.

Let's take a closer look at these reasons.

The government will take care of me.

A couple of years back, I read a report that Washington State's single biggest expense was the Department of Social and Health Services (DSHS). It was the first year that DSHS surpassed education as the State's biggest expense. DSHS and Medicaid is the federal and state welfare system that can help people pay for care. Remember this system is welfare. So you need to qualify based on your health and finances.

Your health has to be very bad, and your money has to be gone before you can qualify for this program. Some exceptions exist to this rule, so if you hire the right attorney, you may get around the "rules." Personally, I have ethical issues with that type of planning. Many people feel they are entitled to a government handout and will do anything possible to tweak the system so the burden of responsibility is shifted from the individual to the taxpayer. Don't get me wrong. I'm glad we have a safety net for those who need it, but it is not okay for people to abuse the system.

Congress recently took up the long-term care challenge with the healthcare reform legislation passed in 2010. A little known provision within the legislation allows the federal government to begin offering long-term care insurance costing somewhere in the range of $100 to $250 per month depending on your age. The premium will be automatically deducted from your paycheck. After you have met the vesting period and paid premiums for five years, you will be able to draw on your insurance coverage in the event you qualify for long-term care. Qualifying usually means meeting the requirements outlined in the policy, which in most private policies requires that you need help with two of the activities of daily living (ADLs) or have a severe cognitive impairment that is expected to last more than ninety days.

ADLs include:

- Eating
- Bathing
- Dressing
- Toileting
- Transferring
- Maintaining Continence

The benefit is expected to provide at least $50 per day to help offset the cost of long-term care. According to the *Genworth 2010 Cost of Care Survey*, the national median daily cost of nursing home care is $206.

Traditional private long-term care insurance companies help reduce their costs and risks by underwriting their policies to require applicants to prove they are healthy so they don't insure those who already need long-term care. This new government program won't require you to pass any type of health screening. It's a great program for people who have been diagnosed with a disease like Multiple Sclerosis or Parkinson's and have a high probability of needing care. I imagine those folks will sign up as soon as this coverage becomes available. On the flip side, some people will be rightly concerned that without requiring underwriting, the payout ratio will increase.

Insurance today works by spreading the risk among a large pool of people, and the insurance companies try to make sure most of the people getting coverage are fairly healthy. If only the unhealthy sign up for this new coverage, then the premiums people are paying may not be enough to cover the costs associated with this program. Because all of the details for this coverage are still unclear, I can't tell if the coverage will be worth the premium or not.

I don't believe this new government-created plan is designed to replace private long-term care insurance but rather to help supplement it. The dust has not settled on how this new coverage will work, but some advantages and disadvantages do exist with it, so you will need to keep a close eye on it.

In the meantime, if you are healthy and can afford insurance premiums, please don't let this new government program stop you from purchasing a good old fashioned private long-term care policy. I am of the opinion that you should always hope for the best, but plan for the worst.

My parents never needed long-term care.

Insurance companies are in business to make a profit. They are not going to offer insurance to people who already require care. They are not going to offer insurance to people who are likely to need care. Insurance companies have developed very sophisticated systems for evaluating your health and the risk of you needing care. They check your medical records and review all of the prescription medications you take. They do in-home health screening and phone interviews to check your cognitive ability. They are going to scrutinize your health thoroughly, and then they will only accept the healthiest people to reduce their risk of paying claims. Insurance companies are very smart at reducing their exposure to this risk.

However, whether or not your parents needed LTC is not a major factor in evaluating you for risk. When you apply for life insurance, the companies want to know all about the life expectancy of your mom, dad, brothers, and sisters. In life insurance, a direct correlation between life expectancy and your heritage exists, but not with LTC insurance.

So maybe your folks needed care or maybe they didn't. Either way, that is not relevant to whether or not you may someday need it.

If I need care, my kids can take care of me.

Some people have children who are registered nurses and doctors, and they have an extra home on their property, so they plan for Mom and Dad to move in if they ever need care. Heck, why not?

They love their parents. They have the care-giving expertise and a special home on their property just for this need. But that is not the case for most of us. In fact, most of us have a romanticized view of growing old.

You may even be thinking, "When I get old, I hope I can move in with my kids and spend my time playing with the grandkids, helping out with the dishes, and reading and gardening to my heart's content." But what happens when your health starts to fail? Do you really want to place a care-giving burden on your family?

Do you want your children to have to bathe you? Do you want your kids to help clean you after you go to the bathroom, or worse do you want them to have to clean up the sheets because you weren't able to make it to the bathroom? Do you want your kids to be up all night with you because of your dementia while you wander around the home and can't remember who your children are?

Is that the type of legacy you want to leave? Do you want to be remembered for the last three to ten years of your life as the decrepit old person who needed twenty-four-hour care, and to bring your children to tears when they remember about the care they provided? Or do you want to be remembered as the supportive caring parent who provided for and loved his or her children?

When asked, most kids say they plan to care for their parents should something happen. Most kids will even try to provide the care. But after months or years of having to lift Dad out of bed, they develop back problems, not to mention anxiety and stress issues. You can't realistically expect your 125-pound daughter to move your 185 pounds. You need to consider the ability of the caregiver to do those everyday things, and how comfortable you'd be if your caregiver were a family member or a friend. My wife cared for her mom in this capacity for several months. While the children are very concerned and want the best for their parents, it's very difficult work physically and emotionally, even in the best situations. Being a caregiver by itself is hard enough, but caring for a person you love is even harder.

Please understand; care-giving is a burden you will be placing on your family in your time of need if you don't make other provisions.

When you own long-term care insurance, you and your family will have more options. Your children can still be involved in your care, but it can be on their terms, rather than their feeling obligated and stuck with no way out. I don't know about you, but I buy insurance to protect the people I love. I own life insurance to replace income and pay off debt if I die. I own disability insurance because if I can't work, I want my family to be able to buy groceries and meet our obligations. I own health insurance, car insurance, and homeowner's insurance because I want to protect my family from the loss associated with these items. Insurance is about protecting the people you love. Sure your kids can take care of you, but do you want them to?

I exercise and eat right so I will never need long-term care.

I believe taking care of your health will greatly reduce your likelihood of needing long-term care. I too eat right and exercise three times a week. I ran the Seattle marathon in 2002. I value good health and strive to make my health a priority in my life, but even though I am healthier than most people I know, I still own health insurance.

Long-term care insurance is an extension of health insurance. It just pays for a health issue after your regular health insurance will no longer pay for the ongoing care you may need. Eating right and exercising will likely increase your life expectancy. My hope is that taking these steps will help ward off your ever needing care. Heck, I wish no one ever needed long-term care. But the reality is that it happens to the best of us. It happens to the healthiest of us.

I have a client who developed dementia in his early eighties. He was a vibrant and healthy engineer. Dementia and Alzheimer's are ugly diseases that can strike even the healthiest people, and a host of other diseases may strike you regardless of how healthy you currently are. He had no idea he would develop dementia, and you don't know that you won't develop it as well. You should plan to be prepared for the possibilities you can't predict.

Long-term care insurance is too expensive.

One of the biggest misconceptions about long-term care insurance is that it's too expensive, but it is actually quite cheap when compared to the cost of actually needing care. If you are sixty years old and married, then a good policy, today, for you and your wife combined, will cost between $3,500 and $5,500 per year for LTC insurance or between $1,800 and $3,000 per person per year for coverage. That may sound expensive compared to your homeowner's insurance, but when compared to the cost of long-term care, the insurance is a bargain.

Today, the average cost of care in the state of Washington is about $200 dollars per day in a facility. For a month, it would be $6,000, and for a year about $72,000. Those numbers are in today's dollars. The cost of care is only going to go up in the future, and it will likely double to $144,000 for facility care in twenty years.

Which one would you rather pay: twenty years of premiums at $4,000 per year, or $12,000 per month for a total of $144,000 per year for the actual care? Medicare reports that once you turn age sixty-five, you have a 40 percent chance you will require some assistance before you die—that's a very high probability. The average length of time that care is needed is 2.8 years. Imagine you had a 40 percent probability your house would catch on fire. Would you go without homeowner's insurance? The chance of your home catching on fire is about 1 in 1,200. The chances of you needing long-term care are 2 in 5. Long-term care insurance will be more expensive to own than homeowner's insurance because it is much more likely to be needed so it is a more expensive risk to the insurance company.

I will never go to a nursing home. I want to stay in my own home.

Most people want to stay in their own homes as long as possible. My family had a family member who was in his mid-nineties when he finally needed care. We were having a hard time providing the care he needed in his home, so we thought he would be better off in a facility. We moved him to a facility, and were paying around $6,000 per month for a very nice private room. After a few less than desirable events, we decided to bring him home because we were not satisfied with the level of care he was receiving. To have the same level of around-the-clock nursing care at home cost us around $9,000 per month. Anything is possible, if you have the money to pay for it.

If you tour a nursing home and ask how many of the residents had planned to end up there, they will all tell you they never thought they would end up there. The good news is your options for your care are expanding. You could receive all of your care in the comfort of your home. Most insurance policies today will pay for care in either your home, in assisted living facilities, or in nursing homes. Just be sure when buying a policy that it will provide for you in your desired place.

I have enough money so I will self-insure the risk.

This excuse is probably the most ridiculous one I have ever heard. Buying long-term care insurance has nothing to do with whether you can pay for your care, and it has everything to do with denying you will ever need the care. If you have enough money to self-insure against the risk of long-term care, then you also have enough money to cancel your homeowner's insurance, knowing that if your home burns down, you could afford to pay for it out of your savings. Or you could cancel your health insurance because if you need major medical care, you could likely cover the cost.

Maybe you can afford to self-insure, but do you really want to risk the expense? You worked your entire life to accumulate what you have, so then, when it's all said and done, do you want to transfer all or a large portion of your wealth to a care facility? Every day you worked hard and saved while others spent like crazy so that one day you would have a large nest egg; do you really want to spend it all on old age care?

If you have enough money to self-insure, then it certainly makes sense to use a small portion of the interest you earn every year to protect the entire nest egg. It comes back to protecting the people who are important to you. If you don't have any family and don't have any church or organization that would benefit from your lifetime of hard work, then by all means please don't buy insurance. Just go ahead and write out the check to the nursing home today.

The good news is that the insurance companies have created hybrid products for people who don't want to "waste" their premium dollars on insurance they will never need. For example, a life insurance policy is now available that has a long-term care rider on it, so if you ever need long-term care, you can access the death benefit to help offset those costs. If you never need long-term care, then you know you didn't waste the premium dollars because your heirs will receive the life insurance proceeds.

An annuity is also available that helps provide leverage for those who want to self-insure. With an annuity, you deposit $100,000, and then you can choose either a two-time or three-time leverage that guarantees to pay you a minimum of 3 percent interest every year and gives you $200,000 or $300,000 to pay for long-term care, depending on the options you choose. These annuities are great because if you plan to self-insure anyway, they allow you to "have your cake and eat it too." You may as well leverage up those same dollars by using one of these hybrid tools.

Generally, if you have less than $2 million in liquid assets, long-term care insurance makes good financial sense. We insure every other aspect of our lives and our health, but for some reason, we overlook an event that has a 40 percent probability of happening. That's kind of silly if you think about it. Unfortunately, most people don't start thinking about or planning for long-term care insurance until one of two things happens: They start to see their health change, and think, "Oh, I better get some insurance just in case, or they start seeing a friend or a loved one go though the long-term care process. When you see someone go through this process, you feel the impact it has on a family. You get a little dose of reality and start to think, "Boy, I never want to put my family into that type of situation."

Long-term care insurance is very hard to qualify for. You have to be very healthy to get coverage, so many times when people finally start thinking about long-term care insurance, they just aren't healthy enough to qualify for coverage. A woman once called me and said she was interested in speaking with someone who could help her decide whether long-term care insurance was appropriate. When she wasn't willing to come to the office, I asked whether I could make a trip out to her house. I explained to her that you have to be pretty healthy to qualify for coverage; she said she was very healthy. Health I have found, however, is relative. When I arrived at her home, she was hooked up to oxygen and was sitting in a wheelchair. But this woman considered herself pretty healthy when compared to her friends. Insurance companies will decline coverage for a lot less than being in a wheelchair and on oxygen. I have seen people declined for high blood pressure in combination with sleep apnea.

Long-term care insurance just makes good financial sense. So when should you buy it? You should buy it as soon as you can afford it without changing your lifestyle. The younger you are, the cheaper it is. If you can buy a policy in your early or mid-fifties, then that would be great. Often, people are still paying for their kids' colleges in their mid-fifties so, from a planning perspective, try to have a policy in force by the time you turn sixty. Another and probably more important consideration is your health. You have to be very healthy to qualify for long-term care insurance. Generally people don't get healthier as they get older, so the younger you are, the more likely you will qualify health wise.

If insurance is the way to go, which company should I choose?

Let's assume you have come to the conclusion that you don't want your family or friends to be your caregivers, and you realize the cost of care is high, but you don't want to pay for it out of your savings. You would rather transfer the risk to an insurance company. Let's also assume you are in pretty good health and you have the finances to be comfortably able to afford long-term care insurance premiums without changing your lifestyle. You are ready to shop for insurance.

Whatever you do, work with an independent agent. You want someone who can help you find the best policy for you. Find a company that is A-rated or better by AM Best. Make sure the company has been in the long-term care insurance industry for at least fifteen years. Find out how many lives it covers. At a minimum, you want a company that insures a minimum of 100,000 thousand people and preferably 500,000 or more. Find out about price stability. Has the company ever increased premiums on its existing book of business, and if so, how many times has it done so? Finding a company that meets all the above criteria is getting harder and harder.

DESIGNING COVERAGE

Designing coverage will require you work with someone who is capable of listening to your concerns. You want to build a policy around your financial situation, not just buy a cookie cutter policy. A good planner will want to know details about your family, finances, and health so he or she can put together a plan to fit your objectives and protect your family.

Once you have your long-term care insurance in place, you may never need to use it—frankly, I hope you don't, but you can sleep well at night knowing that if the situation arises, you will be taken care of without being a burden on your family physically or financially. To get an idea of how much long-term care insurance premiums cost try the website **www.LTC-Expert.com**.

Chapter 12

PAYING OFF DEBT VS. SUPERSIZING YOUR RETIREMENT INCOME

When my son Oliver was just about two years old, we lived in a two-story home where our stairs went down about three steps, came to a platform, turned, went down another seven steps, hit another platform, turned and then went down the final three steps. I would stand on the first platform and Oliver would run and jump to me, flying over the three steps, and I would catch him. He would laugh, I would laugh, and I would swing him around and give him a big hug.

Then one day I was carrying some laundry down the steps in the dark. I had just stepped down onto that first platform when all of a sudden I heard the pitter patter of little feet running in the dark. I turned around just as Oliver took flight. I dropped all of the clothes and did my best to catch him. Somehow, he managed to fly past the first platform and was on his way down the longer flight of steps. I grabbed him by the ankle and we both ended up lying face first, facing down the stairs. Of course, he was crying, but fortunately, he wasn't hurt. We were both very scared. My heart was pounding as I held him. I felt so bad.

The next day I stood on that platform and looked at him. He got a little sparkle in his eye and started to run toward me, but just before it was time to jump, he stopped. It's a horrible feeling to have started a game that resulted in my son falling down the stairs. It's an even more horrible feeling to have had a relationship where there was 100 percent trust and to see that trust damaged because of my mistake.

I do the best financial planning I can for my clients, but despite my best efforts, sometimes things don't go as planned. The sinking sensation in my gut when I dropped my son is the same feeling I get when I see people receiving bad advice, or when I make an error in assessing a situation.

THE RISK OF PAYING OFF DEBT

Getting out of debt is incredibly smart and not using credit is brilliant. But does it ever not make sense to pay off debt?

Frank and Marge came to see me about getting the most out of their retirement income. As I reviewed their income, assets, and liabilities, I learned they were both seventy years old and still had a mortgage. The mortgage was well over $130,000, and they had about $150,000 saved in retirement accounts. Frank and Marge were not the typical folks I meet with, but they were very nice and came to me by referral so I really wanted to help them. As I continued into our discovery meeting, I found out they didn't have enough income to live comfortably every month and they had a fairly large mortgage payment.

Frank and Marge explained to me that they had refinanced their home about two years ago, and they currently had a 4.75 percent rate on their thirty-year mortgage. They were also paying an extra $300 per month toward the mortgage to pay it off early.

Remember, retirement is all about cash flow, not net worth. While I am certainly a proponent of being debt-free, it didn't make sense for this couple to make these extra payments toward their principal. They told me they didn't have enough current income to live comfortably, and an extra couple of hundred dollars a month would really have a significant impact on their existing lifestyle.

Should you try your hardest to get your debt paid off? Absolutely, but don't do it at the cost of your retirement years. I know it's wonderful not to have any debt, and I hope by the time you are retired, you don't have this concern. But is it worth making extreme sacrifices that won't likely benefit you? No.

Let me give you another example of how paying off your debt can hurt your retirement. I met with Barb and Michael whom I believe were given some bad advice. These particular folks were both eighty-six, had grown children, and had been raised during the Great Depression. Because of their upbringing, Michael and Barb always disdained debt. They had worked hard, raised two daughters, put them through college, helped their girls buy cars, and given them down payments for their first homes. They had done everything they could to be financially responsible and to help their children, and then at age seventy, they were tired and ready to retire.

They had been business owners of modest means and had only their social security income. At the time they had retired, they had saved about $100,000 and owed $80,000 on their home when someone told them to take their life savings and pay off the remaining $80,000 mortgage. These folks, not liking debt, thought that was a great idea.

When Barb and Michael came to see me, they hadn't had a mortgage payment in years. They had a car that was twenty years old and in need of a lot of repair. The small $20,000 nest egg they had left over after paying off the mortgage sixteen years earlier had gradually been spent between a few small trips, miscellaneous home and car repairs, and the increasing cost of living. They were now eighty-six years old with no debt, and unfortunately, not enough income. They could barely survive, let alone thrive in retirement. So what could they do now?

Have you ever heard the saying "different strokes for different folks?" Retirement planning is never a "one size fits all" and what works wonderfully for some folks is absolutely the wrong concept for others.

I suggested that Barb and Michael consider selling their home or take out a reverse mortgage on their home. I know many people initially recoil from the idea of a reverse mortgage, but it can creatively solve financial issues for certain people. Let me give you an example of how it could help another couple.

REVERSE MORTGAGES

Let's look at a hypothetical example of how a Reverse Mortgage could be used to help you increase your retirement income and be sure to leave a legacy to your heirs. Mr. Moon is seventy and Mrs. Moon is sixty-eight years old. They are in very good health and have been retired for almost fifteen years. When they retired, their pension was more than enough to cover all of their living expenses. During the last fifteen years, they have seen their medical costs rise substantially, their property taxes increase, and the cost of living increase, which has eaten away at their modest retirement savings. So now they are feeling an income pinch. Mr. Moon is considering going back to work, and they have been taking aggressive steps to cut their expenses. In fact, they are driving a car that is twenty years old, they have canceled their cable television, and they are considering not taking all of their prescriptions to try and save a few extra dollars.

Before Mr. and Mrs. Moon retired, they had paid off their home. Their home is by far their largest asset, and if they had to sell it today, they could probably sell it for $300,000. They think selling their home would free up the capital they would need to live more comfortably. So they start looking to downsize. Unfortunately, what they find is that even the smaller decent homes in nice neighborhoods are going for around $300,000, so they will only break even. They do not want to move into an apartment; in fact, they don't want to move at all. They have lived in the same home for more than thirty years, and they have a lot of wonderful memories, an incredible garden, great neighbors, and they are comfortable.

When I talked with Mr. and Mrs. Moon, I asked them whether they had ever considered using a reverse mortgage. They said yes, but they didn't like it because they have two children, and it was important for them to leave something to the kids. I asked whether the kids would want to live in the home. They said no, the kids would probably sell it and split the proceeds. Leaving a financial legacy to their children was important to them, but leaving the home to the children was not as important. So I asked them this question, "How much would you like to leave to each of your children?" After a little discussion, they came up with $100,000 for each child.

At our second appointment, I asked the Moons whether they would be interested in a solution that would increase their income by about $700 per month and also guarantee that each of their children would receive a $100,000 inheritance. There was no hesitation and an emphatic YES.

For this particular couple, we were able to use a reverse mortgage to generate a guaranteed income stream of $1,000 per month for the rest of their lives as long as they lived in their home. From that $1,000, we used $302.14 to buy a second-to-die guaranteed universal life insurance contract that would pay an income-tax-free death benefit of $200,000 upon the death of the second spouse with each child listed as a beneficiary at 50 percent each or $100,000 for each of their two children. The guaranteed death benefit was to age 110, so it is highly unlikely they would outlive the insurance contract. This leaves them with $697.86 per month to make ends meet.

Now as with any planning, advantages and disadvantages exist, and you should consider all of the different what-ifs, costs, and risks. While this type of planning is certainly not appropriate for everyone, it obviously accomplished the desired goals for Mr. and Mrs. Moon and might also be an option for Michael and Barb, who had paid off their home and now are at risk of losing their retirement lifestyle due to lack of retirement income.

A Final Note

THRIVING IN RETIREMENT

I sure appreciate your taking the time to learn about some of the different ideas, concepts, and strategies I use to help my community and clients transition into and through retirement. I feel blessed to have some of the best clients in the world.

With 10,000 baby boomers retiring every day, and with all of the turmoil we are experiencing in our country and around the world, my hope is you will be able to take some of these concepts and implement them into your own life so they will give you a greater sense of confidence and direction as you transition through this great time of your life.

Yogi Berra once said, "If you don't know where you are going, any road will take you there."

Conversely, when you have a written plan for achieving your retirement goals, you will be much more confident in where you are, where you are going, and how you will get there. I like what Peter Drucker once said, "The best way to predict the future is to create it."

If you are getting ready to retire or are already retired, then I invite you to contact me. My contact information is provided on the last page of this book. I will provide you with a road map for achieving your retirement goals and also provide you with a second opinion about your current retirement plan.

I can't invite everyone I meet to be one of my clients, but I can usually help point out some key issues that can dramatically improve their situations. Occasionally, I meet with people who have their entire financial lives in excellent order, and I can't provide any added value. When that's the case, it's nice to shake their hands and say, "Job well done." But that is the exception, not the rule.

Finally, I'd like to leave you with this one last thought. Many people spend their entire lives in the land of someday. Someday I'll travel, someday I'll retire, someday I'll spend more time with my loved ones, someday I'll write my memoir, and then all of a sudden, something happens. An accident or health event occurs and life changes, and "someday" becomes a lost dream that will never happen. I like the quote by James Oppenheim, "The foolish man seeks happiness in the distance; the wise man grows it under his feet."

May you grow happiness under your feet.

All the best,

Jason Parker

THE PARKER FINANCIAL DIFFERENCE

INDEPENDENT AND CLIENT FOCUSED

Parker Financial is independently owned and has no outside shareholders or corporate ownership. That means our clients' interests are second to none, enabling us to recommend suitable financial products from the whole of the market rather than select areas of the market chosen by corporate interests.

SPECIALIZING IN RETIREMENT

Your life, your health, your family, and your retirement are very serious matters. At Parker Financial, we believe the greatest and most capable hands for these matters are your own hands. Our focus on retirement will aid you in making the wisest and most informed decisions for your future.

WEALTH PRESERVATION

Will Rogers once said, "I am more concerned with the return of my money than the return on my money." Most of our clients shift from a wealth accumulation mindset to wealth preservation in retirement, yet they need to keep an emphasis on long-term growth so their wealth is keeping pace with inflation. By taking a holistic approach to wealth management and focusing on risk mitigation, we incorporate our clients' goals to create strategies that keep their money growing not just for their lifetimes, but hopefully, for many generations to come.

FEE-BASED

In a traditional Commission-Based model, financial advisors do not receive compensation unless they sell a registered product or affect a security transaction. Therefore, when securities are bought and sold, the client pays commission fees. With a Fee-Based structure, financial advisors charge an all-inclusive annual fee for portfolio construction advice, ongoing investment recommendations, and portfolio transactions. Since the financial professional is paid an annual fee for providing services on the client's behalf, there are no additional fees to generate transactions. With no hidden costs, this model serves our clients' best interests.

FIDUCIARY RESPONSIBILITY

Registered Investment Advisors are subject to a fiduciary standard which may be defined as the following: A fiduciary responsibility is an obligation to act in the best interest of another party. A fiduciary obligation exists whenever the relationship with the client involves a special trust, confidence, and reliance on the fiduciary to exercise his discretion or expertise in acting for a client. A person acting in a fiduciary capacity is held to a high standard of honesty and full disclosure in regard to the client and must not obtain a personal benefit at the client's expense.

LOCALLY OWNED

Being a locally owned, community-minded firm that provides institutional-quality investment management services is a great advantage to our clients. Understanding our local community, being involved in volunteer efforts, committee participation, and philanthropic contributions all serve to develop and maintain a long-term relationship with our clients and their families.

ParkerFinancial LLC
Registered Investment Advisor

Jason R. Parker, President
9057 Washington Ave NW #104
Silverdale, WA 98383
www.parker-financial.net
www.thriving-in-retirement.com
360.337.2701
info@parker-financial.net

ABOUT THE AUTHOR

Jason Parker is the founder of Parker Financial LLC, a fee-based registered investment advisory firm specializing in wealth management for retirees. His office is in old town Silverdale, WA 98383. Jason grew up in the foothills of Northern California where he attended and graduated from Heald Business College in Racho Cordova, California with a degree in business administration. Shortly thereafter he moved to Juneau, Alaska where he worked for several years at a small bank and then for a short time at the Alaska Commission on Post Secondary Education. Jason has more than ten years of experience in the financial services arena including banking, insurance and investments. He holds the series 65 securities license as well as being licensed to offer life and health insurance in Washington State.

In addition to being a Certified Retirement Financial Advisor™ (CRFA™), Jason is a respected investment advisor, insurance professional, and business leader in Kitsap County, Washington. He is a member in good standing with the National Ethics Bureau, Better Business Bureau, and the Silverdale Chamber of Commerce. Jason works with a small group of private clients, and he is a well-known financial strategist, speaker, and educator. He is the host of the popular radio program *Sound Retirement Radio* broadcast on 1400am KITZ on Saturdays at 8 a.m. He is also a regular article contributor to the *Kitsap Peninsula Business Journal.* He specializes in working with retirees who share the common values of faith, family, community, integrity and honesty. Jason lives in Poulsbo, Washington with his wife, Rebecca (married since 1997), and their two children. You can visit him at:

www.thriving-in-retirement.com